THE
EVERYTHING

WITHDRAWN

GUIDE TO

COOKING FOR CHILDREN WITH AUTISM

Dear Reader,

Being a parent is tough but rewarding work! It means doing all that you can to make things better for your child. When your child has special needs, this work often includes a variety of different therapies, treatments, and interventions. Many parents of children with autism disorder turn to a gluten- and casein-free diet as one of their interventions.

We know that making changes to your family's diet can be daunting and often overwhelming. We set out to provide you with tips, information, and a collection of easy, healthy, and economical recipes. Once you have these, you may realize that starting a diet that steers clear of gluten and casein doesn't have to be that difficult and can even be a fun way to introduce new foods to your family routine.

We hope that you discover you can satisfy all family members' appetites with great gluten- and casein-free recipes. We have included options for breakfasts, entrees, desserts, and snacks to help you plan your weekly menus. We've even tried to provide you with options for special occasions such as holidays and school activities.

We hope that *The Everything® Guide to Cooking for Children with Autism* provides you with the tools you need to make the transition to gluten- and casein-free eating as easy and fun as possible.

Happy Cooking!

Kim and Megan

D1105076

Welcome to the EVERYTHING Series!

These handy, accessible books give you all you need to tackle a difficult project, gain a new hobby, or even brush up on something you learned back in school but have since forgotten. You can choose to read from cover to cover or just pick out information from our four useful boxes.

 Alerts

Urgent warnings

 Facts

Important snippets of information

 **Essentials**

Quick handy tips

 Questions

Answers to common questions

When you're done reading, you can finally
say you know **EVERYTHING**®!

PUBLISHER Karen Cooper

DIRECTOR OF ACQUISITIONS AND INNOVATION Paula Munier

MANAGING EDITOR, EVERYTHING® SERIES Lisa Laing

COPY CHIEF Casey Ebert

ACQUISITIONS EDITOR Brett Palana-Shanahan

DEVELOPMENT EDITOR Brett Palana-Shanahan

EDITORIAL ASSISTANT Hillary Thompson

EVERYTHING® SERIES COVER DESIGNER Erin Alexander

LAYOUT DESIGNERS Colleen Cunningham, Elisabeth Lariviere,
Ashley Vierra, Denise Wallace

Visit the entire Everything® series at *www.everything.com*

THE EVERYTHING®

WITH AUTISM

From everyday meals to holiday treats—
200 tasty recipes your child will love to eat

Megan Hart, MS, RD and Kim Lutz

Avon, Massachusetts

An Everything® Series Book.
Everything® and everything.com® are registered trademarks of F+W Media, Inc.

Published by Adams Media, a division of F+W Media, Inc.
57 Littlefield Street, Avon, MA 02322 U.S.A.
www.adamsmedia.com

ISBN 10: 1-4405-0021-5
ISBN 13: 978-1-4405-0021-3

Printed in China

J I H G F E D C B A

Library of Congress Cataloging-in-Publication Data
is available from the publisher.

This publication is designed to provide accurate and authoritative information with regard to the subject matter covered. It is sold with the understand-
ing that the publisher is not engaged in rendering legal, accounting, or other
professional advice. If legal advice or other expert assistance is required, the
services of a competent professional person should be sought.
     —From a *Declaration of Principles* jointly adopted by a Committee of the
American Bar Association and a Committee of Publishers and Associations

Many of the designations used by manufacturers and sellers to distinguish
their products are claimed as trademarks. Where those designations appear
in this book and Adams Media was aware of a trademark claim, the designations have been printed with initial capital letters.

This book is available at quantity discounts for bulk purchases.
For information, please call 1-800-289-0963.

This book is dedicated to all the families that are blessed with a child with autism. As these families know, children with autism are amazing individuals who inspire and challenge us.

Our goal for this book was to provide quality information about a complicated diet to those families searching for alternative treatments for their child. Specifically, Megan dedicates it to Nikki, Matt, Sammy, and Maddy. Kim dedicates it to Jason and all the kids from Steve Lutz's classes at Agassiz School in Chicago.

Acknowledgments

Thanks to everyone who inspired us and helped this project be successful. Thanks again to our amazing and supportive husbands. Andy was a super dad and husband who planned many outings for himself and Mason so mom could work on the book, he kept the supply of caffeine up in the house, and acted as technical support with some computer issues! Steve was the taste tester extraordinaire, entertainer for the children, and supreme cheerleader.

Our children, Evan, Casey, and Mason, kept us levelheaded and laughing throughout this book. They also acted as great taste testers for these kid-friendly dishes. Immense gratitude and love to our families. Specifically, Kim's amazing sister, Laura, and her many parents: Ilene and Jeff, Jeff and Alice, Kenny and Silvana, Eileen, and Barbara. Megan sends love and thanks to her parents and Andy's parents: Marlene and Paul, Roz, and Russ and Barb. She thanks all her wonderful siblings and their families, Maureen, Kathy, Dan, and Anne. Megan also wants to thank her godmother, Sondra, who taught her all the secret family recipes. Thank you to all our extended families, in-laws, nieces, and nephews who have also provided us a tremendous amount of love and encouragement.

Thanks to our many friends who encouraged us, provided us with support, taste testing, child care, and input into the creation of this cookbook.

Thanks to Gina Panettieri who brought us this exciting opportunity.

Contents

Introduction

The incidence of autism is on the rise. Families are looking for traditional and alternative resources to help their child and families. This has led more and more parents to try a gluten- and casein-free diet for their child with autism. Many families report an improvement in autism-related symptoms and behaviors when they have removed casein and gluten from their child's diet. Casein and gluten are both proteins found in certain foods.

Making the change to a gluten- and casein-free diet involves thinking about food in a whole new way. Planning and preparation are the keys to success. Gather support around you and your family as you embark on this new diet. Accept that it is a complicated diet that will take some time to learn and adapt to. You will make mistakes learning this diet, and that is okay at the beginning! Strategies for success include menu planning, stocking your pantry with essentials, and jumping into the diet by trying out new recipes. Once you have these items accomplished, you will find that the transition to this diet is not nearly as difficult as you might have expected at the beginning.

The Everything® Guide to Cooking for Children with Autism provides a strong foundation for anyone trying the diet for the first time. There is an emphasis on easy-to-find and readily obtained ingredients in each of the recipes. When specialty ingredients are used, they are kept as basic as possible. For example, there are a wide range of gluten-free flours available to experiment with once you have committed to the gluten- and casein-free diet. These flours are fun to experiment with and provide a broader range of options. However, in this book, gluten-free all-purpose flour is used in place of wheat flour for all baking and cooking recipes that call for flour. When you are just starting out, it is easier on your pocketbook and culinary skills if you stick with a basic, gluten-free all-purpose flour. Once you are comfortable, go crazy and experiment with all the fun flours that are available!

Learning to bake gluten- and casein-free involves learning a whole new science of baking. Gluten is the substance in wheat flour that "binds" or holds baked goods together. Flour that does not have gluten lacks this binding agent. Therefore, gluten-free baking requires the addition of a binding agent, such as xanthan gum or guar gum. The recipes in this book use a gluten-free all-purpose flour that does not contain either xanthan gum or guar gum. If you are using a gluten-free flour that already has the binding agent included as an ingredient, omit the xanthan gum from the recipe.

In addition to providing you with the tools you will need to prepare nutritious, delicious, gluten- and casein-free meals for your family, this book will also provide you with information about how to read food labels and grocery shop. Learning these skills will help to ensure that what you are preparing is, in fact, free of gluten and casein. It is important to think about all of the ways that gluten and casein can find their way into your child's diet so that you can be prepared to prevent unintentional exposures. There are tips throughout the book to help you keep a safe food environment for your child. Tips are included that address daily issues such as grocery shopping, cooking and food preparation, handling parties and school, and cleaning up your kitchen and pantry.

All children need a nutritious diet to grow and thrive. When your child is following a limited diet, such as the gluten- and casein-free diet, having access to sound nutritional information is even more important. *The Everything® Guide to Cooking for Children with Autism* provides basic information that you need to ensure that your child is receiving the optimal nutrition on this diet. Importantly, due to the limited nature of this diet, your child should be monitored by a physician in order to keep track of growth and risks of nutritional deficiencies.

Also because helping to prepare food can be pivotal in getting your child to eat it, this handy cookbook calls out which recipes would be appropriate to cook with your child. You'll see a chef's hat icon 🍳 next to each recipe name that your child can help prepare.

Best of all, though, *The Everything® Guide to Cooking for Children with Autism* will bring joy to your kitchen with recipes for comfort foods and yummy treats including Chicken Noodle Soup (page 61), Chocolate Coconut Brownies (page 229), and the fabulous Taco Dinner (page 132). Have fun discovering reinvented versions of old favorites and new delights. With helpful hints, strategies for success, and delicious recipes, this book will help you make the transition to a gluten- and casein-free diet with ease.

CHAPTER 1

Autism and Diet

The relationship between diet and autism is an exciting and emerging science. Many families choose to investigate the effects that dietary changes may have on their child with autism. It is important to know that changes in diet do not cure autism but offer one possible option to help manage the symptoms of the disorder. The goal of this book is to provide families with safe and reliable information about the gluten- and casein-free diet. More importantly, this book offers families safe, cost-effective, nutrient-rich, and healthy options for those following the gluten- and casein-free diet.

Autism 101

Autism is a complex neurobiological disorder that typically lasts throughout a person's lifetime. It is part of a group of disorders known as autism spectrum disorders (ASD). Today, autism is more common than pediatric cancer, diabetes, and AIDS combined. It occurs in all racial, ethnic, and social groups and is four times more likely to strike boys than girls. Autism impairs a person's ability to communicate with and relate to others. It is also associated with rigid routines and repetitive behaviors, such as obsessively arranging objects or following very specific routines. Symptoms can range from very mild to quite severe.

How many children and families are affected by autism? The latest research from the Centers for Disease Control (CDC) indicates that 1 in every 150 children has autism. This means that 560,000 children are affected with this disorder in the United States. Autism does not just affect the child diagnosed. It is a life-altering condition that affects every member of the family and social circle of that child. The CDC defines autism spectrum disorder as follows:

> *Autism spectrum disorders (ASDs) are a group of developmental disabilities defined by significant impairments in social interaction and communication and the presence of unusual behaviors and interests.*

 Question

What is the difference between autism disorder and Asperger's syndrome?
These diagnoses are available in the *DSM-IV* through the American Psychiatric Association. Briefly, to be diagnosed with autistic disorder a child must have impairments in social interaction and communication and exhibit repetitive patterns. A diagnosis of Asperger's syndrome is similar to autism; however, these children do not have as many issues with verbal communication.

What Causes Autism?

Every child is unique and amazing. Children with autism are no different; their autism disorder gives them many unique and interesting characteristics that endear them to their families and friends. Parents want to help their children succeed and be able to interact with their family and peers. One of the hardest realities of autism is that, currently, there is no known cure. Treatments exist to help lessen the symptoms and severity of the disease but no definite cure has been identified. The medical community has also been unable to identify the true cause of autism at this time. This makes for a complicated situation.

The research regarding the cause of autism disorder is confusing and studies oftentimes contradict each other. Some researchers believe that the cause of autism is genetic only. Others believe that there is a genetic component to this disorder and also some type of environmental trigger that causes this disease to emerge. These environmental causes are not well understood. There are many theories about which environmental factors may trigger the emergence of autism, but most are still being studied.

 Fact

The earlier the diagnosis is made, the earlier interventions can begin. Currently, there are no effective means to prevent autism; however, there are several treatments. Symptoms and severity can be minimized with intense early intervention. Research indicates that early intervention in an appropriate educational setting for at least two years during the preschool years can result in significant improvements for many young children with autism spectrum disorders. Effective programs focus on developing communication, social, and cognitive skills.

Therapy for Children with Autism

Autism research is relatively new. This fact makes it very difficult for families to find reliable and trustworthy information. Families can find an overwhelming amount of information on the Internet and in the media, but oftentimes this information is conflicting. It might take a little time to find the right treatment options for your family and your child.

Currently, the primary goal for therapy is to improve a child's development throughout his or her lifespan. According to the American Academy of Pediatrics, the educational interventions that help children with ASD provide children with structure, direction, and organization. It is important to individualize therapy for each child's own individual needs.

A team approach is helpful to identify and tailor the therapy to meet the developmental needs of the child as well as capitalize on the specific strengths of each child. Many children have an array of doctors, behaviorists, occupational therapists, speech and language pathologists, music therapists, holistic practitioners, acupuncturists, dietitians, teachers, and specialists on their team.

 **Essential**

Research on the Internet can be overwhelming. It is difficult to know where to start searching for information on autism and the treatment options for autism. Here are some reliable sites to start with: Autism Speaks: *www .autismspeaks.org*; American Academy of Pediatrics: *www.aap.org/health topics/Autism.cfm*; and Centers for Disease Control: *www.cdc.gov/ncbddd/ autism.*

When children are diagnosed, many families begin to search for cures and therapies to help. One alternative therapy that is very common for many families to consider is specific changes to their child's diet. Dietary intervention in autism is still considered a complementary and alternative therapy. It is important to meet with a dietitian or physician trained in the specifics of this diet. This is a restrictive diet; you want to have accurate information, and your child should be followed closely on this diet to ensure proper growth.

Dietary Intervention for Children with Autism

The most common form of dietary intervention in children with ASD is the gluten- and casein-free diet. In 2007, a study published in the *Journal of Autism and Developmental Disorders* showed that 54 percent of families identified as using complementary and alternative medicines used dietary changes as a therapy for autism. This diet is widely used even though the connection between the diet and the effects on the child are still being studied.

The gluten- and casein-free diet impacts all aspects of your child's diet, so it is important to talk with your physician before beginning a trial of the diet. Due to the restrictive nature of this diet, it is important to closely monitor children's growth and nutritional health while following this plan. Discuss with your physician about tracking your child's response to this therapy.

Communication and teamwork are vital for the success of this diet. Work with your treatment team to determine when and how to start the diet. It is also important to communicate with your treatment team about how long to try out this diet. Some children will respond quickly, others take slightly longer, and still others show no response to this diet. Defining certain start and end points at the beginning can make complying with the diet easier.

The Medical Community and the Gluten- and Casein-Free Diet

Parents want to give their children the best of everything. When your child is diagnosed with autism, that desire only intensifies. Families of children with autism want to provide every opportunity to improve their child's symptoms. One of the first things people look into when researching their possible options is the gluten-free and casein-free diet.

This diet has received a lot of attention, and there are many websites dedicated to promoting the diet as the cure to autism. It is important to know, however, that the current medical research is limited on the benefits of a gluten- and casein-free diet in children with autism. Most of the information available on the gluten- and casein-free (GFCF) diet has been testimonials from parents and teachers claiming that the diet has resulted in behavioral improvements in their children. Other people report that the diet has improved physical conditions, such as constipation or other gastrointestinal (GI) complaints, in their children. In medical studies, typically, the number of subjects in the study is small, which makes it harder to infer that the results will be the same for a large group of children with autism. It is an area of great interest in the medical community. Hopefully, research will continue to further the science behind the diet and other medical interventions to move closer to a cure for autism.

The bottom line is that this diet is not the cure for autism; however, it does offer families hope. Certain children respond to this diet in a positive way, others have no response, and many others are somewhere in between. Many families do decide to try the diet to evaluate where their child falls in this spectrum.

The Latest Medical Research about This Diet

The medical community looks for research-based studies before making conclusions about the success of medical therapies. Research in dietary intervention in children with autism is very limited and is just at the beginning stages. Conflicting reports exist in the medical literature.

The Journal of Autism and Developmental Disorders published a randomized double-blind clinical trial using the GFCF diet in children with autism in April 2006. This research study was conducted with only fifteen subjects. This study did not show any statistically significant changes in autism-like behaviors; however, several parents did report improved symptoms. The small number of children in this study was a limitation. Studies need to be conducted on a larger scale.

To date, the studies conducted on the GFCF diet in autism have been inconclusive, but most have shown promise. It is clear from the research that the need exists for larger and properly designed studies of the possible benefits of this diet in children with autism.

The Connection Between Autism and Diet

Proponents of this diet claim that the diet can affect a child with autism in a multitude of ways. Families report that children with autism have an increased level of interaction after starting on the diet. Sleep and eye contact are reportedly improved. Stooling patterns and issues with constipation and diarrhea have become less of a problem. Again, each child's reaction or nonreaction to this diet is unique.

A behavioral therapist can help to track your child's individual response to the diet. This data is not published in medical journals, but may help an individual family track their child's response or lack of one to the diet.

Behavioral Connections

How can a diet cause changes in behavior? There are a few different theories that are proposed to link autism behavior with diet. It is important to note that these ideas are only theories and none of these have been proven. Many people have proposed different ways that the diet of a child with autism may affect behavior.

 Alert

In the 1960s, a researcher named Dohan noticed that the population of the South Pacific Islands had lower rates of schizophrenia. Upon further investigation, it was noted that the population of these islands also consumed a diet mostly free of gluten and casein. A correlation was made between a gluten- and casein-free diet and lower rates of mental illness. During this time of early research, this diet became popular as a treatment to manage the symptoms of this mental illness.

One of the most popular theories of how the gluten- and casein-free diet relates to autism is often called the "leaky gut theory." This particular theory was made popular by a researcher named Reichelt. His research indicates that people with autism have a certain defect (specifically, a lack of a particular digestive enzyme) in their gastrointestinal tract that allows certain proteins to pass into the bloodstream. These proteins are thought to cause changes to the way the brain functions.

What does this mean? Under normal digestion, the proteins gluten and casein are broken down from large proteins into smaller proteins or peptides. These peptides are then further broken down by the digestive enzymes in the gastrointestinal tract into the smallest proteins, which are called amino acids. Typically, it is these amino acids the body is designed to absorb into the bloodstream and utilize for all necessary functions.

How is this potentially different in a child with autism? The theory is that in the gastrointestinal tract of people with autism, the proteins from gluten and casein are indeed broken down and digested into peptides. However, people with autism may have difficulty breaking these peptides further down into amino acids. The theory is that they might be lacking the digestive enzyme to break the protein down from peptides to amino acids.

What happens? Their bodies will readily absorb the whole peptides through the "leaky gut" instead of waiting until these are broken down into amino acids. Therefore, a child with autism may have whole peptides in their bloodstream. In multiple studies, the prevalence of this increased gut permeability has been reported in 40–70 percent of children with autism. The body is not used to receiving the proteins in this form and cannot process them correctly.

Why does this matter? These peptides have a similar chemical structure to opium or heroin and are sometimes called opioids. It is possible these peptides could end up crossing the blood-brain barrier and act like opioids in the brain. These opioids are thought to cause some of the behavior changes seen in autism.

Theoretically, by removing these whole proteins from the diet, the body may have less accumulation of these opioid-like peptides in the bloodstream. Therefore, less opioids cross into the brain. This could possibly result in fewer autism-like behaviors. This link is still unproven but is an emerging area of research in the medical community.

Response to the Gluten-Free and Casein-Free Diet

How long does a person need to be on this diet until results are seen? There is no specific information about how long the diet needs to be followed in order to see results. Results are highly variable, poorly understood, and still being studied. Reports vary from a few days to a few months until results are seen. The specific changes reported from parents and researchers vary: changes in behavior, changes in skin rashes, improved bowel movements, better sleeping, and improved attention and interactions with family and therapists. Importantly, some children do not see any changes on this diet. Just as your child is unique, his or her response to therapies will be unique and individual.

Gastrointestinal Abnormalities

Gastrointestinal (GI) disturbances can be defined as any symptom that relates to problems with the stomach, gastrointestinal tract, and digestion or absorption of food and nutrients. Many children with autism do have trouble with their bowel movements and often report having digestive issues. In one study, about 30–40 percent of children with autism have some reports of gastrointestinal disturbances.

Changes in Stool

One of the most common symptoms in children with autism is trouble with bowel movements. Children with autism can struggle with constipation, diarrhea, and abdominal pain. There can be both a medical component and a behavioral component to a child's bowel issues. Any changes in a person's diet can affect bowel movements. It is possible that changing to a GFCF diet can lead to increased intake of fruit, vegetables, and fiber, which may help to regulate the stool pattern of a child on the GFCF diet. These improvements may allow a child to come off certain medications used to help stimulate bowel movements.

Gastroesophogeal Reflux

Another common GI issue is gastroesophogeal reflux. One study indicates that a large percentage of children with autism have reflux and inflammation in the gut and esophagus. A combination of reflux and esophageal inflammation can cause pain, which may not be identified in a child with autism because expressing pain is sometimes difficult. It is possible that if these children are unable to express the pain that they feel due to GI discomfort, their behaviors and self-soothing behaviors may be intensified.

Changes to the diet can lead to decreased pain and inflammation associated with gastroesophogeal reflux. Theoretically, it is possible that if changes to the diet lead to less irritation, this may lead to less self-soothing behaviors as a result of decreased pain and irritation. This is one example of how this diet can affect behavior. This is not a well-studied area of this diet and this information is mostly theoretical.

Bacteria in the Gut

It has been well documented that children with autism have an abnormally high level of bacteria in the gut. Treatment for this high level of bacteria varies from antifungal medications to changes in diet to oral supplements of high doses of probiotics, or a combination of all these treatments. There are not yet any good medical studies showing how to treat these abnormal levels effectively. Furthermore, it is not well understood if treatments targeted toward lowering these bacteria are effective in changing behaviors or relieving gastrointestinal symptoms.

Popular Dietary Changes

The gluten- and casein-free diet is the most popular dietary change for people with autism, but it is not the only one considered. Many alternative therapies for autism exist. Families often try combinations of the many treatments to determine which is going to help their child. Changes to the diet are often the first line of defense that families use to try to treat autistic behaviors. Each family and each child is unique, and there are many options for families. Treatments should be tailored to the specific family and child. What works for one child and family may not work for others. Families need to support each other in their individual choices and not pressure each other to adopt their beliefs and strategies.

Food Allergies

Food allergies are increasing in the general population and, therefore, are on the rise in children with autism. Many families choose to pursue allergy testing for their children with autism to screen for potential food allergies. A child with special needs may require special testing procedures to help identify these allergies. If your child does have specific food allergies, the only treatment is complete removal of those allergens from the diet.

However, if you are considering trying the GFCF diet as a therapy to alleviate autism-related behaviors, allergy testing will not indicate whether it will be of benefit. The theories behind behavioral changes and the GFCF diet, as mentioned above, are separate issues from food allergy. This means that a child who is not allergic to milk or to wheat might still benefit from a gluten- and casein-free diet.

Organic Lifestyle

Organic eating and supporting an organic lifestyle is on the rise. The organic lifestyle is becoming more and more popular as a method to better care for the planet and our families. The effects of some food manufacturing techniques and the amount of pesticides used in the food supply is a concern for families. One way to limit your family's exposure to pesticides is to change to an organic diet. Choosing organic foods is becoming easier and easier in our grocery stores. Organic eating can often be combined with other dietary changes and diet therapies. Many families choose to follow an organic gluten- and casein-free diet.

 **Essential**

The way to determine if a product is organic is to read the label. Read carefully! Products labeled "100 Percent Organic" are made entirely from organic ingredients or components. Products that are made up of at least 95 percent organic ingredients or components, and have remaining ingredients that are approved for use in organic products, can display the "USDA Organic" seal. Products that are made up of at least 70 percent organic ingredients or components can list "organic" before those ingredients on their ingredient lists.

Additives, Colorings, and Preservatives

Another dietary change that some families choose is to limit their child's exposure to certain food additives, colorings, or preservatives. Although not well documented in medical literature, some families report positive changes in behavior and sleep patterns when these items are limited. Food additives have long been associated with changes in children's behavior, and children with autism are no different in that regard. Most of the dietary changes recommended for children with autism also limit the presence of food additives, colorings, and preservatives. The gluten- and casein-free diet encourages more whole food consumption, which may also contribute to improved behavior by limiting these additives and preservatives in your family's diet.

CHAPTER 2

Good Nutrition on a Gluten- and Casein-Free Diet

G ood nutrition is important for every child. Providing good nutrition can also be a parent's greatest challenge. Typically, the GFCF diet is tried shortly after diagnosis of autism during the toddler years. Toddler eating is challenging in general, but the challenge is intensified in a child with autism. It requires consistency as well as some creativity to meet the needs of a growing toddler on the gluten- and casein-free diet.

Special Concerns for Special Children

Children with autism disorder have several unique traits that can make dietary changes difficult to implement. Children with autism have difficulty accepting changes to their routine or comfort zone. They also struggle with accepting new foods or new food textures. These create unique opportunities and challenges for families looking to implement this diet. The most important thing to remember is to capitalize on your child's strengths and work together to overcome barriers. It may take multiple attempts and different trials in order to be successful. Be patient with yourself and your child.

Food Selectivity in Children with Autism

Multiple studies on children with autism have shown that they often limit the food that they eat. There are many reasons for this behavior. One of the features of autism is a limited interest in new experiences. Children with autism also enjoy repetitive behaviors. Both of these components of autism can lead to limited food selection.

Children with autism can also resist new experiences such as trying new foods. Furthermore, children with autism can have sensitivity to different textures, and this can limit the foods they accept. All of these behaviors can make it difficult for a child to meet his or her nutrition needs. It can also make it difficult to start and be successful with a very restrictive diet such as the gluten- and casein-free diet.

Nutrient Deficiencies

Studies have been conducted to try to identify which nutrients children with autism are at risk for deficiency. The studies have been conflicting. One study by Herndon in the *Journal of Autism and Developmental Disorders* showed that children with autism actually consume more vitamin B_6, vitamin E, and protein that is nondairy. They also showed that children with autism take in less calcium and dairy than children without autism. Both children with and without autism in the study had low intakes of fiber, calcium, iron, and vitamin D. Of note, these children were not on the gluten- and casein-free diet.

Eliminating foods containing gluten and casein removes two of the main staples in the typical diet. It removes many of the grains that are frequently eaten in our culture and also dairy products or prepackaged foods that contain dairy protein. By removing these basic components of the diet, it is important to look at what micronutrients are being taken out of the diet. It is important to note that typically much of our grain and bread products are fortified with iron and B vitamins; however, the gluten- and casein-free bread products are often not fortified with these nutrients.

Removing dairy from the diet also limits the most popular sources of calcium and vitamin D in the diet. Therefore it is important that your child take a gluten- and casein-free multivitamin each day to help meet his or her nutritional needs. Also, additional calcium and vitamin D supplements are often needed. When using a milk alternative, ensure that it is fortified with calcium and vitamin D. Please meet with your doctor or dietitian to discuss what vitamin and mineral supplements would benefit your child while on this restrictive diet.

 **Essential**

Nutrition goals for children based on the Recommended Daily Allowance (RDA): Children age one to three years old need about 1,300 calories, 11 grams of protein, and 500 milligrams of calcium per day. This increases as they age and children four to six years old need about 1,800 calories, 15 grams of protein, and 800 milligrams of calcium per day.

What Can My Child Eat on the GFCF Diet?

The beginning of the gluten- and casein-free diet is overwhelming and can seem impossible. Removing these items from your family's diet can make it feel like there is nothing left to feed your family. This diet does require a major lifestyle change, but remember that there are still plenty of foods available to choose from. The initial stages of this diet are the toughest, but once you learn how to choose and prepare gluten- and casein-free meals and snacks, it becomes easier and easier to incorporate this into your lifestyle. If your child responds to the diet, the benefits will often outweigh the difficulties of the diet.

A person on the gluten- and casein-free diet can still enjoy most meats, beans, potatoes, corn, rice, fruits, and vegetables. Also, there are many gluten- and casein-free products available in grocery stores and online to allow your family to still have some of the items that you might feel that you are missing on the gluten- and casein-free diet.

The table on page 16 shows some staples to stock the pantry with when starting on the gluten- and casein-free diet. Keep these ingredients on hand to make most of the recipes in this cookbook.

STAPLES IN A GFCF FAMILY PANTRY

Grains and Dried Beans	Produce and Meat	Oils, Sauces, and Seasonings	Baking Goods
Brown rice	In-season fresh produce	Olive oil	GF all-purpose flour
Arborio rice	Onions	Canola oil	Xanthan gum
Quinoa	Garlic	GF vegetable bouillon	Brown sugar
Cornmeal	Avocado	GF chicken bouillon	Baking powder
Polenta	Banana	GF chicken broth	Baking salt
Lentils	Dried blueberries	GF beef broth	GF oats
Dried black beans	Lemons	GF barbecue sauce	Cornstarch
Dried pinto beans	Limes	Light agave nectar	GFCF bread crumbs
Flaxseed meal	Beef	Honey	GF vanilla extract
Whole flax seeds	Chicken	GF Dijon mustard	GFCF marshmallows
	GFCF hot dogs	GF mayonnaise or vegonaisse	GFCF peanut butter
	GFCF breakfast meats	Pure maple syrup	Sunflower seed butter
			Potato flour
			Oat flour

Canned Goods	Frozen Foods	Breads/Cereals	Dairy Products
Beans: black, pinto, cannellini, kidney	Frozen berries	GFCF bread	GFCF soy milk
Diced tomatoes	Frozen mangoes	Corn tortillas	GFCF sour cream
Sunflower nut butter	Frozen spinach	GF Rice Chex	GFCF soy yogurt
Canned pineapple	Frozen broccoli	GF Corn Flakes	GFCF cheese
Canned pumpkins	Frozen mixed vegetables	GFCF bagels	GFCF cream cheese
Light coconut milk	Frozen chicken breasts	GFCF pasta	Eggs
GFCF marinara sauce	Frozen fish portions		GFCF margarine
Hominy	GFCF waffles		GFCF ice cream

The world of grains and rice is still available on the gluten- and casein-free diet. Many different flours and grains are gluten free. It might be fun to try out some new grains and see which ones your family enjoys!

Here is a list of gluten-free and casein-free flours that are *safe* to choose:

SAFE FLOURS ON THE GFCF DIET

Acorn	Almond
Amaranth	Arborio rice
Aromatic rice	Arrowroot
Basmati rice	Brown rice or brown rice flour
Buckwheat	Calrose
Canola	Cassava
Channa	Chestnut
Chickpea	Corn, corn flour, corn gluten, corn malt, cornstarch
Cottonseed	Dal
Dasheen flour	Enriched rice
Fava bean	Flax or flax seeds
Garbanzo	Glutinous rice
Hominy	Instant rice
Job's tears	Millet
Modified cornstarch	Modified tapioca starch
Montina	Peanut flour
Potato flour or potato starch	Quinoa
Red rice	Rice, rice bran, and rice flour
Risotto	Sago
Sesame	Sorghum
Soy or Soya	Tapioca
Teff	

As you become more comfortable with the diet and cooking gluten and casein free, try experimenting with different flours and grains. The fun aspect of this diet is that you can be as adventurous as you want with trying different flours, grains, and specialty products.

What Does My Child Need to Avoid on the GFCF Diet?

First, what are gluten and casein? It is easier to identify foods and products that contain these proteins if you understand what they are! Gluten is a special protein that is found in wheat, rye, barley, bulgur, Kamut, spelt, and foods made from those grains. Gluten gives breads and grains their texture. It is often used as a filler in meat products like hot dogs and lunchmeat. Gluten is found in food starches, semolina, couscous, malt, some vinegars, soy sauce, flavorings, artificial colors, and hydrolyzed vegetable proteins. Casein is a protein found in milk and foods containing milk. These include cheese, butter, yogurt, ice cream, whey, and many brands of margarine. It also may be added to nonmilk products such as soy cheese and hot dogs in the form of caseinate.

 Question

Are all "soy" or "dairy-free" products gluten- and casein-free?
No! This cookbook uses a lot of soy products (i.e., soy cheese and soy milk) but it can be hard to find truly casein-free soy dairy products. Many of them contain caseinate, so it is imperative to read labels carefully! Often, these items can be special ordered online, or your local grocery store may be able to order a supply to keep in stock. Appendix A at the back of the book has a list of resources that make it easier to locate GFCF foods.

The List

Below you will find a list of ingredients to avoid, as they indicate the presence of gluten and casein. It is important to look for words such as these on all food ingredient labels. Check for words like these every time you shop. Manufacturers change their ingredients often, so you do need to check the label *each time* you grocery shop.

UNSAFE INGREDIENTS ON THE GFCF DIET

Abyssinian Hard (wheat triticum duran)	Acidophilus milk
Artificial butter flavor	Avena or wild oat
Baking powder and soda (read labels, may be okay)	Barley
Barley malt or barley extract	Barley Hordeum vulgare
Beer, ale, or any fermented beverages	Blue cheese (contains gluten and casein)
Bran	Bread flour
Broth (may contain wheat)	Bouillon (There are some GF bouillons—read labels!)
Bulgur	Butter
Butter fat, butter flavoring, butter oil	Buttermilk
Calcium caseinate	Caramel colorings
Casein	Caseinates
Cheese (hard and soft)	Cereal, cereal extract, or cereal binding
Chilton	Chorizo (check label)
Coffee Creamers and coffee creamer substitutes	Cottage cheese
Couscous	Cracker meal
Cream	Cream cheese
Cream yogurt	Croutons
Curds	Custard
De-lactosed whey	Dextrin
Dinkle	Durum
Einkorn wheat	Emmer
Faro	Farina
Flavorings, natural or artificial (need to check with manufacturer)	Filler
Fu (dried wheat gluten)	Flours (all purpose, barley, bleached, bread, brown, durum, enriched, gluten, graham, granary, high-protein, high-gluten, oat, wheat, whole meal, and white)
Galactose	Germ
Glutamate	Glutamic acid
Gluten	Graham flour
Gravies, prepared with gluten and casein, check labels	Gum base

UNSAFE INGREDIENTS ON THE GFCF DIET

Half and half	Hard wheat
Hydrolysates with casein	Hydrolyzed oat starch, hydrolyzed plant protein, hydrolyzed vegetable protein, hydrolyzed wheat gluten, and hydrolyzed wheat protein
Kamut	Lactalbumin and lactalbumin phosphate
Lactic acid (need to verify source)	Lactoglobulin
Lactose and lactulose	Magnesium caseinate
Malt, products including beverages, extracts, milks, flavorings, syrup, and vinegars	Matzo or matzah flour and/or meal
Milk (condensed, evaporated, dry, whole, low-fat, nonfat, skim, and goat's)	Milk protein, milk powder, milk solids
Miso	Modified food starch (check with manufacturer as might be wheat)
Mustard powder	Oats that are not gluten-free oats (It is possible to order gluten-free oats in the Untied States)
Oriental wheat	Orzo
Panko	Potassium caseinate
Pudding	Rennet casein
Rice malt, rice syrup, and brown rice syrup	Rye and rye semolina
Sauces (check labels)	Seitan
Semolina	Sodium caseinate
Sodium lactylate (check with manufacturer)	Sour cream, sour cream solids, sour milk solids
Soy sauce (may contain wheat)	Spelt
Starch, edible	Stativa
Triticale and triticum	Udon noodles
Wheat, wheat bran, and wheat germ, wheat germ oil, wheat grass, wheat starch, and whole-wheat berries	Whey (all forms)
Whey protein	Yogurt

This list of unsafe foods can be overwhelming. Take time to read it, copy it, and take it to the grocery store each time. Please remember that you do not have to memorize this list, just take a copy with you while shopping and read the labels. After some time on the diet, the list will become familiar and comfortable.

Hidden Sources of Gluten and Casein

Certain foods are easy to identify as safe or unsafe. Others might be a little trickier. These items might also contain gluten or casein and it may require a little more research to determine if the food is safe. Please read the labels of these items carefully to eliminate those that contain gluten and casein from your family's lifestyle. It might be necessary to call the phone number on the back of the product and ask the manufacturer the sources of some of these ingredients. If they are not from a gluten or casein source then they are safe to consume.

POSSIBLE SOURCES OF GLUTEN AND CASEIN

Breadings	Over-the-counter medication
Brown rice syrup	Play dough (You can find great gluten- and casein-free recipes for this on the Internet.)
Candy	Prescription medications
Coating mix	Roux
Communion wafers	Sauces
Gloss and balms	Self-basting poultry
Herbal supplements	Soup bases
Imitation bacon/seafood	Stuffing
Lipstick	Thickeners
Luncheon meats or vegetarian meat substitutes, certain types	Vitamin and mineral supplements
Marinades	

How to Read Food Labels

Learning how to read food labels is a survival skill on the gluten- and casein-free diet. It is important for you to check the labels for unsafe ingredients each time that you purchase a food item. Manufacturers are often changing formulas and manufacturing techniques.

Following is an example of a food label. The top portion provides valuable information about the nutrition content of the food. It includes information on serving size, calories, fat, protein, and micronutrients such as vitamins A and C, calcium, and iron. The information at the top of the food label, although valuable, will not tell a person if the food is safe on the gluten- and casein-free diet.

The biggest help in deciding if a food is safe or unsafe is the ingredient list. Review the list of ingredients and compare it to the safe and unsafe lists provided in this chapter. The items are listed by weight in the product from greatest to least. The first ingredient in the list is the largest component of the food and the last ingredient is the smallest component in the food. Just because an item is last in the list, which means there is a small amount, does not make it safe. If an unsafe ingredient is anywhere on the list, it is an unsafe food.

 Fact

If a food label claims that the food is "gluten free," it does *not* mean that the food is truly gluten free. The law is still being finalized to define "gluten free." It is important to check the ingredient list each time you buy the food, and it might be necessary to call the manufacturer about cross-contamination at the plant.

A Food Label Test

Look at the food label on page 23. Is this a safe food on the gluten and casein-free diet? Review the label and compare it to the list.

Nutrition Facts	Amount/serving	%DV*	Amount/serving	%DV*
Serv. Size 1 cup (249g)	**Total Fat** 12g	**18%**	**Sodium** 940mg	**39%**
Servings About 2	Sat. Fat 6g	**30%**	**Total Carb.** 24g	**8%**
Calories 250	Polyunsat. Fat 1.5g		Dietary Fiber 1g	4%
Fat Cal. 110	Monounsat. Fat 2.5g		Sugars 1g	
*Percent Daily Values (DV) are based on a 2,000 calorie diet.	**Cholesterol** 60mg	**20%**	**Protein** 10g	**20%**
	Vitamin A 0% • Vitamin C 0% • Calcium 6% • Iron 8%			

INGREDIENTS: WATER, CHICKEN STOCK, ENRICHED PASTA (SEMOLINA WHEAT FLOUR, EGG WHITE SOLIDS, NIACIN, IRON, THIAMINE MONONITRATE [VITAMIN B1], RIBOFLAVIN [VITAMIN B2], AND FOLIC ACID), CREAM (DERIVED FROM MILK), CHICKEN, CONTAINS LESS THAN 2% OF: CHEESES (GRANULAR, PARMESAN AND ROMANO PASTE [PASTEURIZED COW'S MILK, CULTURES, SALT, ENZYMES], WATER, SALT, LACTIC ACID FROM WHEY, CITRIC ACID AND DISODIUM PHOSPHATE), BUTTER (PASTEURIZED SWEET CREAM [DERIVED FROM MILK] AND SALT), MODIFIED CORNSTARCH, SALT, WHOLE EGG SOLIDS, SUGAR, DATEM, RICE STARCH, GARLIC, SPICE, XANTHAM GUM, CHEESE FLAVOR (PARTIALLY HYDROGENATED SOYBEAN OIL, FLAVORINGS AND SMOKE FLAVORING), MUSTARD FLOUR, ISOLATED SOY PROTEIN AND SODIUM PHOSPHATE.

Is it safe? No!

Some of the ingredients that are not safe are the following: enriched pasta (containing semolina wheat flour), cream, cheese, lactic acid from whey, butter, and starches. Read carefully each time you buy a food!

 Alert

Always check the ingredient list! Manufacturers often label products as "wheat free." This does not mean that it is gluten-free. A food that is wheat free can still contain gluten. Similarly, if a food is lactose-free or milk-free, it does not mean that it is casein-free. Please check the ingredients list *each time* a food is purchased! It is the only way to make sure that a food is safe!

Starting the Gluten- and Casein-Free Diet

After reading these lists, some families decide that the gluten- and casein-free diet is too overwhelming to go forward. Many others are ready to jump right into the full diet, and still others take their time easing into this lifestyle change. The important thing is to recognize that, despite the lifestyle changes required to be successful with this diet, it really can be done!

It is important to plan out the start of this diet. You do not have to start it immediately after deciding that this might be something to try with your family. Gather books on the diet, build some ideas for recipes, join support groups in your area or find online support groups to help encourage you in this endeavor. Prepare yourself for success.

How to Get Started

There is no right or wrong way to go about this: What works for your family is the correct way to enter the diet. Each family has a different personality, and they know what will work for them. Some people jump right in without a transition period. Others prefer a more gradual transition to the diet and start with small changes, building up to the full diet.

If a slower transition is wanted, one way to accomplish this is to first start with eliminating casein from your family's diet. Go to the grocery store and purchase different casein-free products. Try some new recipes that are casein-free. Gather some casein-free alternatives to milk and begin to try them out to see which milk substitutes your child and family accepts and enjoys. Realize that eliminating the gluten and casein from your diet will change the texture of some of your favorite foods. Look to expand into new favorite foods rather than try to recreate gluten- and casein-free versions of your favorite foods.

After you have been successful at eliminating casein, venture into the full gluten- and casein-free diet. Some people choose to start by changing one meal, for example, breakfast. Try a week's worth of breakfasts that are gluten- and casein-free. Others choose to use the full diet on certain days of the week and not on others. Again, there is no right or wrong way to make these transitions. It is an individual decision. The goal is to slowly build up your options for breakfast, lunch, dinner, and snacks that are all gluten- and casein-free.

How to Tell If the Diet Is Working

This is one of the hardest questions to answer. The science for this therapeutic diet is still emerging, and to date the results have been mixed. Most outcomes have been reported by parents but have not been proven in scientific journals. There does seem to be a relationship between this diet and changes in behavior for some children with autism. It is important to note that not all children respond to the diet, and not all children who do respond have the same outcome. People report changes in behavior, changes in skin issues, changes in bowel habits, and changes in interactions. It is important to talk to your doctor about starting this diet and monitoring your child while on the diet for adequate growth and development and for any potential nutrition deficiencies that can result from a restrictive diet.

A Typical Day on the Diet

What does a typical day on the gluten- and casein-free diet look like? This diet focuses a lot on what your child and family cannot eat! There really are foods left to eat that can be prepared quickly, economically, and healthfully.

Breakfasts can be gluten- and casein-free waffles with maple syrup or eggs cooked in olive oil and gluten- and casein-free bacon with a side of potatoes cooked in oil. Try the Banana Soy Yogurt Milkshake on page 72. The Breakfast Pizza on page 76 is great for a treat. Orange juice can be enjoyed as a drink or make the Orange Pineapple Smoothie on page 82.

Lunches can be a gluten- and casein-free soup and a gluten- and casein-free muffin with a glass of soy milk. Try making gluten- and casein-free

Chicken Nuggets on page 138 and pair it with the Quinoa and Bean Salad on page 109.

Dinners can be a baked meat or fish, baked potato fries, side of vegetables, and a glass of soy milk. Try the Barbecued Tofu on page 143 and pair it with Cheesy Polenta with Roasted Vegetables on page 147. Try the Baked Honey Pescado on page 126 to give your child a boost of omega-3 fatty acids.

Snacks can be fruit, corn chips, or gluten-free pretzels. Try some fun snacks like the Caribbean Dream Boats on page 164 or the Pizza Toast on page 167. For a cool treat, make the Lemon Raspberry Ice Pops on page 219.

Vitamins, Minerals, Medications

Once your family has mastered the gluten- and casein-free diet, look into other hidden sources of gluten and casein in your lifestyle to eliminate. Gluten and casein are often found in nonfood items. It is important to look at the label of each medication, herbal supplement, vitamin, and mineral that your child ingests. It may even be necessary to call the manufacturer of each of these items to clarify the composition of the ingredients in these products. Manufacturer's information should be on the back of the packaging, and they should be able to provide a full list of the ingredients in their products. Milk protein is often an added ingredient in lotions and cosmetics, as well. This could be a hidden source of casein if your child frequently puts his recently lotioned hands into his mouth.

This diet is restrictive and could lead to nutrient deficiencies if not followed properly. Please consult a physician and a registered dietitian before beginning this diet. Children should be monitored closely while on this diet to ensure they are meeting their growth goals and are not developing nutrient deficiencies. Each child should begin taking a daily gluten- and casein-free multivitamin, along with a calcium and vitamin D supplement, while following this diet.

CHAPTER 3

Strategies for Success

A dvance planning can make the difference between success and frustration when trying to adopt a gluten- and casein-free diet for your child. Knowing how your child's new eating routine will fit into your family life, school experience, and outside activities will allow you to be prepared in all situations with appropriate meals and snacks. Communication within your family and with others with whom your child comes in contact is also a key component for success.

Feeding Your Whole Family

Whether your family consists of just yourself and your child with autism or you have a large family with several children and other adults, everyone needs to feel satisfied with the food they are offered. Changing your child with autism's diet will definitely impact the other members of your family. Finding ways to make that impact a positive experience will dictate whether you are able to stick with the diet for the long run or whether it becomes too burdensome to continue.

Eating Separately

Take advantage of those times when your family is not eating together to provide the family members not following the gluten- and casein-free diet with their familiar and favorite foods. Your other children can bring sandwiches on wheat bread, yogurt containers, and cheese and crackers packed in school lunches. Other adults in the family can eat gluten- and casein-containing foods at work or when the children are at school or at play dates. Family members who are not making the change in diet will not feel cheated if they are still able to enjoy favorite foods away from the family member who is making the change.

One of the most important things to keep in mind is that it is counterproductive to introduce gluten or casein through crumbs or dirty work surfaces. Making the change in diet can be hard work, and the last thing you want is to undermine that effort by inadvertently keeping gluten and casein in your child's diet. Therefore, if you are preparing foods that contain gluten or casein for other members of your family, it is imperative to preserve the integrity of the gluten- and casein-free food-preparation space. Use separate cutting boards and utensils for foods that contain gluten or casein. It is a good idea to get a second toaster or toaster oven to prevent crumbs from mixing. Make sure that all surfaces that might be contaminated with crumbs are cleaned up thoroughly. Use separate sponges or dish brushes when washing dishes that were used for foods with gluten or casein. Remembering to prevent contamination when cleaning up will help your transition to the gluten- and casein-free diet go much more smoothly.

 **Essential**

If a parent date night or a shopping trip to the mall with one of your other children includes eating out, favorite foods can be enjoyed without risk of bringing crumbs with gluten or casein into the kitchen. (There is the added bonus of no cleanup, too!)

It can be helpful for everyone in your household if you keep a supply of foods for the gluten- and casein-free diet in a separate area of a cabinet or pantry. That way, your child can help herself to food or a caregiver can provide a snack confident that the food is part of the diet. It is also extremely important not to introduce gluten- or casein-containing crumbs into jars that are also going to be used for anyone following the gluten- and casein-free diet. For example, you should not put a knife with wheat-toast crumbs into a jar of peanut butter that is then going to be used for a child following the diet. It is a good idea to keep separate jars of condiments for those who follow the gluten- and casein-free diet and those who don't.

Eating Together

Life is busy enough without having to make two separate dinners every night. If you are preparing tasty dishes, there is no reason why the whole family can't enjoy gluten- and casein-free dining. If you're serving yummy pancakes, smoothies, or muffins for breakfast, no one will probably even notice the change. Think about what your family likes now and take those ideas into your new menu planning. For example, if your family loves Mexican food, instead of serving the cheese enchiladas that you've traditionally prepared, try making the Taco Dinner (page 132) from this book that is free of casein and gluten. You might just find a new family favorite without anyone feeling like they're making a sacrifice. Focusing on good flavors and varied ingredients will help ensure success.

Planning ahead is an important strategy for success. In order to ensure good nutrition, following the guidelines set out in Chapter 2, you need to include a wide variety of foods. This is especially important because the gluten- and casein-free diet is a limiting diet that already cuts out several otherwise available foods. Looking at the full day's menu, or even the full week's, will allow you to double-check that your child is receiving a full range of vitamins, minerals, protein, and fiber. For example, a typical day on the gluten- and casein-free diet could include Granola (page 74) with soy milk and fruit for breakfast, a cup of Minestrone Soup (page 64) with gluten-free crackers for lunch, a rice cake with sunflower-seed butter or peanut butter with a cup of calcium-fortified juice for a snack, and Tofu Spinach Lasagna (page 157) with a Green Salad with Mock Caesar

Dressing (page 106) for dinner. Finish it off with a cup of hot chocolate and a dish of fresh berries for dessert and you have a delicious and well-balanced diet for the day.

Communication is just as important as good cooking for your family to buy into the gluten- and casein-free diet. Most parents try the diet for their child with autism with the hope that they will see improvements in troubling behaviors and symptoms. These behaviors and symptoms impact everyone in the household. If you explain the reasons why you are making these changes and enlist the help of other family members, you might well find that they are as eager to give it a try as you are. Throwing in the occasional yummy gluten-free Chocolate Chip Cookie (page 217) won't hurt either!

 Essential

Don't expect gluten- and casein-free foods to taste exactly the same as traditional versions of the same foods. To get a tasty result, many different ingredients are used to attain good texture and flavor in gluten- and casein-free cooking. Try to put expectations aside and experience each dish for the unique creation that it is.

Talking to Family, Friends, and Schools about the GFCF Diet

Every child comes into contact with so many other people every day. Other parents, teachers, caregivers, and other children might all offer your child food throughout the day. Communicating with the people who spend time with your child is extremely important.

Including Diet in the School Plan

Once your child is in school, he will have an Individualized Education Plan (IEP) to ensure that the school is providing the best possible education in light of your child's special needs. Part of the IEP process is an annual review meeting. This meeting can be a great time to discuss the role that diet will play in managing your child's autism.

 **Question**

What if my child's IEP meeting happened before we made the change in diet?
Contact your child's case manager at the school and his classroom teacher. Let them know in writing that you have introduced the diet and what ramifications that will have in the classroom. If you feel you need to amend the IEP, you can request another meeting, but oftentimes communicating with the school in a spirit of collaboration will achieve good results.

Doing some homework before the meeting can make it much easier for school personnel to understand the changes in your child's diet and what they can do to help facilitate it. At the back of this book (Appendix B) is a worksheet that you can complete and bring with you to the IEP meeting. Printing information about the diet from the Internet can also be helpful. Ask your doctor if she has any tools available to bring with you, too. It is then important to make the gluten- and casein-free diet part of the written record of the IEP plan.

Showing school staff that you want to work with them as opposed to against them can make a huge difference in whether they will try to accommodate your child's dietary needs with enthusiasm or reluctance. Providing the school with written ideas for items to take the place of foods containing gluten and casein in the classroom is a good first step to bringing everyone onboard. For example, if little candies or cheesy crackers are traditionally used to help with math and counting activities, suggest using buttons, stickers, or beads. If the teacher rewards good behavior with candy or treats, a reward chart or certificate can be a great, and safe, substitute. Many teachers have been using the same methods for years, and they will need assistance in changing their mindsets. A friendly letter that includes a list of alternatives can take a lot of the pressure off already overworked teachers.

Keep track of what is happening in the classroom. Monitor homework that is coming home and teacher updates about what is happening in the classroom. It can take a little time for a teacher new to the diet to completely understand all of the ramifications that it can play in the classroom. For example, if your child comes home with a necklace made from dried noodles, it is important to remind the teacher about alternatives. A teacher might think that it is acceptable to use foods containing gluten or casein for activities that don't involve eating. However, the risk is great that children might put items not intended for eating into their mouths.

The IEP plan should include what steps to take if there are problems with the diet in school. Once those steps are laid out, it is much easier to know how to best address any situations that arise. Since the IEP process is a collaborative process, the teacher will be able to have input on how he would like to be best alerted to any issues.

 Alert

Most people in your child's life will be happy to help make things easier for you. The key to enlisting that help is information. Explain to family and friends why you are making the change. Teach them the basics of the diet. If your child's grandma knows what is okay to eat and what is not, she will be much more comfortable when the family comes to visit.

Making It Easy on Everyone

When your child is on a special diet, control becomes a very real concern. You will work conscientiously to ensure that your child is not being exposed to gluten and casein, and you don't want him to be exposed accidentally when that can be prevented. Using that desire for control to your advantage can help make it easier for everyone to feed your child.

Entertaining in your home where you are accustomed to following the gluten- and casein-free diet can take a lot of the stress out of larger gatherings of family or friends. You certainly are able to exert the greatest amount of control over what is served if you're doing the cooking. Although this can help in some situations, it's not realistic that you will start hosting every birthday party and holiday in your social circle.

When the festivities are at someone else's house, offer to bring a dish or two. If you bring a favorite dish of your child's, it will be much easier to avoid foods that are off-limits. Explaining your situation to your host can also make a big difference. Many people are happy to add a fruit salad or other gluten- and casein-free treat to the menu if they know that it will make it easier for your family. Talking to your host can mean the difference between stressing out over pretzels or enjoying a couple of potato chips.

 **Essential**

Unlike an allergy, an accidental exposure is not an emergency. For the diet to be optimally effective (or to assess whether it's helpful for your child), it is best to strictly avoid gluten and casein, but if an accidental exposure happens, just make a note of any changes in your child's behaviors or symptoms and go back to following the gluten- and casein-free diet.

If there's no way to bring a dish, pack a little snack bag with foods that are acceptable for the gluten- and casein-free diet. It can also be helpful to feed your child before attending a party where you're not sure what will be served. A child with a full belly and a yummy snack will be a much a happier child than a child who looks hungrily at food that she is not allowed to eat.

Making the Most of Convenience Foods

There is not always enough time in the day to make all of the delicious, nutritious food for your family that you would like. Even on the gluten-free/casein-free diet, there are still many convenience foods that you can use to supplement your child's diet. Choosing healthy entrees, ready-to-go snacks and occasional treats can make it that much easier to stick to the diet when your life gets challenging.

Specialty Items

There has been a veritable explosion in the availability of gluten-free foods. Today, you can get a wide range of gluten-free foods at even mainstream grocery stores. Specialty stores and natural foods stores have an even wider variety. There are also many websites that offer gluten-free foods for purchase. It is important to ensure that not only are convenience foods gluten-free, but also casein-free.

In that category, though, there are many foods available to choose. There are gluten- and casein-free pizzas, crackers, frozen entrees, cookies, puddings, and snacks. Look for foods that are labeled "gluten-free," and double-check the ingredients list. To ensure that foods are casein-free, look at the ingredients list and also look for the "vegan" label on foods. Foods labeled "dairy-free" are not always completely dairy-free and might actually contain casein. Also, "lactose free" indicates an absence of the sugar found in cows' milk, but not the protein (casein).

 Question

Why should I look for foods labeled "vegan" if my family eats meat?
Vegan foods are foods that are prepared without any animal ingredients. Although that means that they don't contain meat or eggs, it also means that they are free of all dairy ingredients. To be consistent with the gluten- and casein-free diet, vegan foods also need to be gluten-free.

Frozen and Prepared Foods

Not only are specialty foods available to help supplement your menu planning, but frozen and prepared foods can make mealtime easier. For example, keeping frozen fruits on hand can make it easy to whip up a smoothie at any time. Most salsas, many jarred pasta sauces, and a wide range of soups are gluten-free and casein-free. Keeping a well-supplied pantry can ease mealtime pressure on overly stressful days.

Feeding Your Child When You're Out and About

A hungry child can quickly become a melting-down child. Being prepared can prevent a tantrum from ever starting. It is a good idea to keep packets of nuts, raisins, or casein- and gluten-free granola bars on hand, either in your bag or in your car, in case you need to feed your child on short notice. In a pinch, you can also get gluten- and casein-free snacks easily when you're out and about. Many convenience stores carry bananas, applesauce cups, and even gluten- and casein-free cereal. In a jam, remember that most potato chips and tortilla chips are free of gluten and casein, as well.

Eating out can be a fun family experience. Some types of restaurants are easier to enjoy on the gluten- and casein-free diet than others. While pizzerias are limiting, Asian food, Mexican food, and Mediterranean food all lend themselves to many options that are consistent with the gluten- and casein-free diet. Rice and corn are gluten-free, and stir-fried or grilled meats and vegetables are readily available. When enjoying Asian food, bring along a bottle of wheat-free soy sauce, and ask the restaurant to use that rather than gluten-containing soy sauce for your meal. As with friends and family, communication is the key to success when dining out. There are resources to help steer you toward restaurants that are more friendly toward people who need to eat gluten-free. Celiachandbook.com has a restaurant guide that is regularly updated. Another online resource is *www.glutenfreerestaurants.org*. Since gluten-free is only one-half of the equation, it is also important to communicate with each restaurant you visit about all of your dietary limits, including the need for dairy-free options.

Holidays and Special Occasions

Food is one of the centerpieces of social gatherings in our culture. That can be challenging when your child is on a limiting diet, such as the gluten- and casein-free diet. Some forethought and planning can make celebrations more joyous for your family.

Birthday and Family Parties

One of the easiest ways to prepare for birthday parties is to bake up a batch of Cupcakes (pages 212–13) and keep them in the freezer. Any time your child has to go to a birthday party, you can thaw one of the cupcakes, frost it, and pack it to go along with your child. That way, when everyone else is enjoying cake, your child can, too.

Once you've explained the reasons for the diet with your family members, many of them might want to help out, too. By sharing favorite gluten- and casein-free recipes with loved ones, you will have a better chance of ensuring there are several safe choices at potluck gatherings. As mentioned previously, you can also offer to host the celebration or to bring a couple of delicious dishes with you to family parties. Remember, people can only help make things easier for you and your child if you let them know how to help.

Halloween

Halloween is a holiday that at first glance seems focused primarily on the mass consumption of chocolate and candy. Broaden your view of the holiday to discover many ways to celebrate this spookiest of days gluten- and casein-free. Consider distributing pencils, stickers, tattoos, or inexpensive toys instead of candy to trick-or-treaters. Not only will you not have a lot of forbidden treats around your house, but you will be providing a safe alternative to other children who also have dietary restrictions. If your child wants to trick or treat, you can make prearrangements with neighbors or friends. If you bring them safe goodies for your little trick-or-treater to request, you can help your child safely enjoy the holiday. Spicy Pumpkin Muffins (page 54) also make a yummy Halloween treat.

Christmas/Hannukah

Making new traditions can be one of the easier ways to make your holidays inclusive for your child following the gluten- and casein-free diet. For example, making safe cookies is a great way to get ready for the holidays. Making decorations and gifts is another food-free fun activity. Instead of chocolate advent calendars, there are several other nonfood holiday countdown decorations that fulfill the same purpose. Gluten- and casein-free candies can take the place of traditional Hannukah gelt and dreidel games. Look for treats and activities that are consistent with your child's diet to set an inclusive stage for family fun. Chocolate Nut Clusters (page 228) and Cranberry Oatmeal Cookies (page 46) might just become new family favorites.

Valentine's Day

It is easy to control the content of what Valentine's Day festivities look like in your own home. Valentine's cards and little gifts can easily take the place of chocolates and candy. Sending your child to school with safe treats—such as stickers, bookmarks, small puzzles, or bubbles—can help you make sure that your child will not feel left out if off-limits treats are also distributed. Chocolate-Coated Strawberries (page 231) and Mixed Berry Muffins (page 52) are great ways to celebrate Valentine's Day with your loved ones.

School Functions

Most parents want to provide a safe environment for all the children in their child's classroom. You can help these other parents help your child by writing a friendly letter explaining your child's situation. A good letter will help other parents understand why your child is following a special diet and what that diet entails. If you give a couple of suggestions of safe treats that everyone can enjoy, you will likely be pleasantly surprised that many potentially difficult situations will be avoided. Ask your child's teacher if you can keep a small supply of safe snacks in the classroom for those times when off-limits treats are provided. It is much easier on everyone (especially your child) if you can take precautions that allow all the children to participate in classroom celebrations.

CHAPTER 4

Homey Baked Goods

Blueberry Apple Muffins

A muffin and a soy yogurt makes a fun and yummy lunchtime meal.

INGREDIENTS

2 cups gluten-free all-purpose flour

1 teaspoon xanthan gum

1½ teaspoons baking powder, divided

½ teaspoon salt

1 cup chunky applesauce, divided

½ cup flaxseed meal

¼ cup coconut oil

¾ cup packed brown sugar

½ cup gluten-free, casein-free soy milk

1 teaspoon gluten-free vanilla extract

1 cup blueberries

1. Preheat oven to 350°F.

2. Lightly oil a standard muffin pan.

3. In a small bowl, combine flour, xanthan gum, 1 teaspoon baking powder, and salt. Stir with a whisk.

4. In a medium bowl, combine ½ cup applesauce with ½ teaspoon baking powder.

5. Add remaining ½ cup applesauce.

6. Mix in flaxseed meal, coconut oil, brown sugar, soy milk, and vanilla.

7. Slowly mix dry ingredients into the wet.

8. Gently mix in blueberries.

9. Spoon batter into oiled pan.

10. Bake 25–30 minutes or until a toothpick inserted into the center of a muffin comes out clean.

MAKES 12 MUFFINS

Calories: 223 | Fat: 7 g | Protein: 3 g | Fiber: 4.4 g

Don't Judge the Muffin by a Lick of the Spoon!

If you're used to baking with traditional ingredients, then you might be used to tasting the batter. When you bake with xanthan gum, though, the batter can have a sour taste. This flavor does not come through in the baked good, however. So trust your recipe, and save the tasting for the finished product.

Cinnamon Soy Cream Cheese Muffins

To make your own oat flour, grind gluten-free, old-fashioned rolled oats in a blender or food processor until it becomes a fine flour.

INGREDIENTS

¾ cup applesauce

2¼ teaspoons baking powder

¾ cup flaxseed meal

⅜ cup canola oil

1½ cups packed light brown sugar

1 teaspoon gluten-free vanilla

¾ cup gluten-free, casein-free soy milk

2 cups gluten-free all-purpose flour

1 cup gluten-free oat flour

1 teaspoon xanthan gum

¾ teaspoon salt

1 cup gluten-free, casein-free soy cream cheese

1½ teaspoons cinnamon

1 tablespoon pure maple syrup

1. Preheat oven to 350°F.

2. In a large bowl, combine applesauce with ¾ teaspoon baking powder.

3. Add flaxseed, oil, brown sugar, vanilla, and soy milk to applesauce mixture.

4. In a medium bowl, whisk together flours, xanthan gum, 1½ teaspoons baking powder, and salt.

5. In a small bowl, combine soy cream cheese, cinnamon, and maple syrup.

6. Slowly stir flour mixture into applesauce mixture.

7. Mix cream cheese mixture into batter.

8. Oil a standard muffin pan.

9. Spoon batter into pan.

10. Bake 25–30 minutes or until a toothpick inserted into the center of a muffin comes out clean.

MAKES 18 MUFFINS

Calories: 258 | Fat: 10 g | Protein: 4 g | Fiber: 4 g

Corny Cornbread

This fluffy cornbread makes a great accompaniment to soup or chili. The corn kernels add an interesting texture.

INGREDIENTS

1 cup cornmeal

1 cup gluten-free all-purpose flour

1 teaspoon xanthan gum

2¼ teaspoons baking powder, separated

1 teaspoon baking soda

¾ teaspoon salt

¼ cup applesauce

⅓ cup agave nectar

1 cup gluten-free, casein-free soy milk

3 tablespoons gluten-free, casein-free margarine

1 cup corn kernels (fresh or frozen)

1. Preheat oven to 400°F.

2. Oil an 8- or 9-inch-square baking pan.

3. In a medium bowl, combine cornmeal, flour, xanthan gum, 2 teaspoons baking powder, baking soda, and salt.

4. In a large bowl, combine applesauce and ¼ teaspoon baking powder.

5. To applesauce mixture, add agave nectar, soy milk, and margarine.

6. Slowly mix dry ingredients into wet.

7. Mix corn kernels into batter.

8. Spread batter into prepared baking pan.

9. Bake 25–30 minutes or until a toothpick inserted into the center of the bread comes out clean.

MAKES AN 8- OR 9-INCH-SQUARE PAN

Calories: 215 | Fat: 4 g | Protein: 4 g | Fiber: 5 g

Zucchini Muffins

You can use store-bought applesauce in this recipe as a timesaver.

INGREDIENTS

3 cups gluten-free all-purpose baking flour

1½ teaspoons xanthan gum

1 teaspoon baking soda

1¾ teaspoons baking powder, divided

1 teaspoon salt

1 teaspoon cinnamon

¾ cup applesauce

1½ cups packed dark brown sugar

¼ cup canola oil

½ cup flaxseed meal

1 tablespoon gluten-free vanilla extract

2 cups raw grated zucchini

1. Preheat oven to 350°F.

2. Oil a standard muffin pan.

3. In a medium bowl, combine flour, xanthan gum, baking soda, 1 teaspoon baking powder, salt, and cinnamon. Stir with a whisk.

4. In a large bowl, combine applesauce with ¾ teaspoon baking powder.

5. Mix in brown sugar, oil, flaxseed meal, and vanilla.

6. Mix in zucchini.

7. Slowly mix dry ingredients into wet, adding one half at a time. Stir until combined.

8. Spoon into oiled muffin pan.

9. Bake 25–30 minutes or until a toothpick inserted into the center of a muffin comes out clean.

MAKES 12 MUFFINS

Calories: 286 | Fat: 7 g | Protein: 4 g | Fiber: 5 g

Enticing the Picky Eater

It can be extremely frustrating if your child has limited his diet to just a few items. Trying new foods, like zucchini, in the guise of a sweet muffin can be a way to broaden your child's diet. When your child won't eat a serving of fruit or vegetables, give muffins a try!

Sweet Potato Muffins

You can use a baked sweet potato instead of canned sweet potato puree for this recipe. Peel and mash a well-cooked large sweet potato until it's smooth.

INGREDIENTS

2½ cups gluten-free all-purpose flour

1 teaspoon xanthan gum

2¼ teaspoons baking powder, divided

¾ teaspoon salt

1 teaspoon cinnamon

¼ teaspoon nutmeg

¼ teaspoon ground ginger

¾ cup applesauce

¼ cup canola oil

1 cup packed brown sugar

1 teaspoon gluten-free vanilla extract

2 tablespoons blackstrap molasses

2 cups sweet potato puree

1. Preheat oven to 350°F.

2. Oil a standard muffin pan.

3. In a medium mixing bowl, combine flour, xanthan gum, 1½ teaspoons baking powder, salt, and spices.

4. In a separate bowl, combine applesauce and ¾ teaspoon baking powder.

5. To applesauce mixture, add canola oil, brown sugar, vanilla, molasses, and sweet potato.

6. Slowly mix dry ingredients into wet.

7. Spoon into prepared muffin pan.

8. Bake 18–23 minutes, or until a toothpick inserted into the center of a muffin comes out clean.

MAKES 12 MUFFINS

Calories: 170 | Fat: 6 g | Protein: 3 g | Fiber: 3 g

Keep Your Cool, Xanthan Gum!

Xanthan gum is a great tool for gluten-free baking, as it helps the nonglutinous flour ingredients stick together. However, you only need a little bit in any given recipe, so one package can last a long time. To maximize the life of your xanthan gum, keep it in the freezer. Well packaged and kept cold, xanthan gum can last for up to six months.

Cornmeal Pizza Crust

*Experiment with different pan sizes
for a thicker or thinner crust.*

INGREDIENTS

4 cups gluten-free, casein-free
vegetable broth

1½–2 cups polenta or coarse-cut
cornmeal

½ teaspoon garlic pepper

½ teaspoon dried oregano

½ teaspoon dried basil

½ teaspoon salt

2 tablespoons olive oil

Lunchbox Ideas

Slices of pizza, soy yogurt and
granola, soup and crackers, or
a dip with vegetables and
gluten-free chips or crackers
are all great lunches to pack for
school.

1. Preheat oven to 425°F.

2. Bring vegetable broth to a boil.

3. Stir in 1½ cups of cornmeal and
   seasonings. Reduce heat to a
   simmer.

4. Continue to stir as cornmeal
   thickens. Cook for 15–20 minutes,
   stirring every minute or two. To
   make mixture thicker, add more
   cornmeal.

5. Spread 1 tablespoon olive oil in a
   9" × 13" jelly roll pan.

6. Spread cornmeal mixture into pan.

7. Brush crust with 1 tablespoon olive
   oil.

8. Bake 20 minutes or until edges are
   browned.

9. Top with sauce and toppings of
   your choice and bake for another
   10–12 minutes.

MAKES 9 PIECES

Calories: 162 | Fat: 4 g | Protein: 3 g | Fiber: 1 g

Cranberry Oatmeal Cookies

If you're craving a tasty cookie but don't have any cranberries on hand, substitute raisins or another GFCF dried fruit.

INGREDIENTS

1 cup gluten-free all-purpose flour

1 teaspoon xanthan gum

2 cups gluten-free old-fashioned rolled oats

½ teaspoon cinnamon

½ teaspoon baking soda

½ teaspoon salt

¼ cup applesauce

¼ teaspoon baking powder

½ cup packed dark brown sugar

¼ cup pure maple syrup

½ cup canola oil

½ cup dried, sweetened cranberries (gluten-free)

½ cup gluten-free, casein-free chocolate chips (optional)

1. Preheat oven to 350°F.

2. Combine flour, xanthan gum, oats, cinnamon, baking soda, and salt in a medium bowl. Stir with a whisk to combine.

3. In a large bowl, combine applesauce with baking powder.

4. Add brown sugar, maple syrup, and canola oil.

5. Mix dry ingredients into wet.

6. Stir in cranberries and chocolate chips, if using.

7. Drop by tablespoon-full onto ungreased cookie sheets.

8. Bake 13–15 minutes or until golden brown. Remove to cooling rack to cool.

MAKES 48 COOKIES

Calories: 73 | Fat: 3 g | Protein: 1 g | Fiber: 1 g

Is Pure Maple Syrup Important?

Yes. Many "pancake syrups" are mixtures of several ingredients. They can include gluten- or casein-containing ingredients. Pure maple syrup comes from maple trees and does not contain either casein or gluten.

Strawberry Cranberry Muffins

If you are going to use frozen strawberries, thaw them and drain off any extra juice before using in this recipe.

INGREDIENTS

2 cups gluten-free oat flour

1½ teaspoons baking powder, divided

½ teaspoon salt

½ cup applesauce

½ cup flaxseed meal

¼ cup canola oil

¾ cup packed light brown sugar

¼ cup orange juice

1 cup chopped strawberries

½ cup dried cranberries

Are Oats Okay for a Gluten-Free Diet?

Check with your doctor before including gluten-free oats in your diet. Oats do not contain gluten, but oats that are not labeled "gluten free" are probably contaminated with other gluten-containing grains through the growing, milling, or packaging process. For many people who follow a gluten-free diet, doctors feel that gluten-free oats are a safe whole grain.

1. Preheat oven to 350°F.

2. In a medium bowl, combine oat flour, 1 teaspoon baking powder, and salt.

3. In a large bowl, blend applesauce and ½ teaspoon baking powder.

4. Mix flaxseed meal, oil, brown sugar, and orange juice into applesauce mixture.

5. Add dry ingredients into wet.

6. Roughly chop strawberries.

7. Mix strawberries and cranberries into batter.

8. Spoon batter into an oiled muffin pan.

9. Bake 30–35 minutes, or until a toothpick inserted into the center of a muffin comes out clean.

10. Remove to a cooling rack and cool completely.

MAKES 12 MUFFINS

Calories: 259 | Fat: 9 g | Protein: 4 g | Fiber: 6 g

Basic Crepes

Making crepes takes a little practice to perfect your flipping technique, but they still taste very delicious while you're working on your style.

INGREDIENTS

¼ cup gluten-free, casein-free soy milk

¼ cup water

2 tablespoons plus 1 teaspoon melted gluten-free, casein-free margarine, divided

½ cup gluten-free all-purpose flour

¼ teaspoon xanthan gum

⅛ teaspoon salt

1. In a small or medium bowl, combine soy milk, water, and 2 tablespoons melted margarine.
2. Add remaining ingredients and stir with a fork until smooth.
3. Brush a 5- or 6-inch skillet with melted margarine and heat over medium-high flame.
4. Pour approximately 3 tablespoons of batter into pan, swirling batter.
5. Once edges are set, flip with a pancake turner and cook on other side.
6. Place cooked crepes on waxed paper to cool.

MAKES 4 CREPES

Calories: 117 | Fat: 72 g | Protein: 2 g | Fiber: 2 g

Maple Cinnamon Crepes

These sweet crepes are perfect for fruit filling. Try filling with all-fruit preserves, Strawberry Applesauce (page 85), or sliced bananas.

INGREDIENTS

¼ cup gluten-free, casein-free soy milk

¼ cup water

2 tablespoons plus 1 teaspoon melted gluten-free, casein-free margarine, divided

1 tablespoon pure maple syrup

½ cup gluten-free all-purpose flour

¼ teaspoon xanthan gum

⅛ teaspoon salt

¼ teaspoon cinnamon

1. In a small or medium bowl, combine soy milk, water, 2 tablespoons melted margarine and maple syrup.

2. Add remaining ingredients and stir with a fork until smooth.

3. Brush a 5- or 6-inch skillet with melted margarine, and heat over medium-high flame.

4. Pour approximately 3 tablespoons of batter into pan, swirling batter.

5. Once edges are set, flip with a pancake turner and cook on other side.

6. Place cooked crepes on waxed paper to cool.

MAKES 4 CREPES

Calories: 130 | Fat: 7 g | Protein: 2 g | Fiber: 2 g

Old-Fashioned Biscuits

This recipe is for drop biscuits, but you can also roll out the dough and cut out the biscuits with a cookie cutter.

INGREDIENTS

2 cups gluten-free all-purpose flour

1 teaspoon xanthan gum

1 tablespoon baking powder

½ teaspoon salt

½ cup gluten-free, casein-free margarine

½ cup gluten-free, casein-free soy milk

1. Preheat oven to 425°F.

2. In a medium bowl, combine flour, xanthan gum, baking powder, and salt.

3. Cut margarine into flour mixture with either a pastry cutter or two knives.

4. Mix in soy milk; use your hands if it is too hard to stir with a spoon.

5. Scoop out egg-size spoonfuls of batter and place on an ungreased cookie sheet.

6. Bake 12–15 minutes or until golden and crusty.

MAKES 6 BISCUITS

Calories: 281 | Fat: 16 g | Protein: 4 g | Fiber: 5 g

Chocolate Chip Mini Muffins

These muffins are a great treat, and their little size makes them easy to take along when you're on the go.

INGREDIENTS

2 cups gluten-free all-purpose flour

1 teaspoon xanthan gum

1 teaspoon baking powder

½ teaspoon salt

½ cup applesauce

½ cup flaxseed meal

¼ cup canola oil

¾ cup packed light brown sugar

½ teaspoon gluten-free vanilla

¼ cup gluten-free, casein-free soy milk

1½ cups gluten-free, casein-free chocolate chips

1. Preheat oven to 350°F.

2. Oil a standard muffin pan.

3. In a medium bowl, combine flour, xanthan gum, 1 teaspoon baking powder, and salt.

4. In a separate medium bowl, combine applesauce with baking powder.

5. Mix flaxseed meal, canola oil, brown sugar, vanilla, and soy milk into the applesauce mixture.

6. Mix dry ingredients into wet, one half at a time.

7. Stir chocolate chips into batter.

8. Spoon batter into oiled muffin pan.

9. Cook 12–15 minutes or until a toothpick inserted into the center of a muffin comes out clean.

MAKES 24 MUFFINS

Calories: 152 | Fat: 7 g | Protein: 2 g | Fiber: 2 g

Mixed Berry Muffins

In summer, substitute fresh berries. Any combination of raspberries, blueberries, blackberries, or strawberries works really well in this recipe.

INGREDIENTS

2 cups gluten-free all-purpose flour

1 teaspoon xanthan gum

1½ teaspoons baking powder, divided

½ teaspoon salt

½ cup applesauce

½ cup flaxseed meal

¼ cup gluten-free, casein-free margarine, melted

¾ cup packed light brown sugar

½ teaspoon gluten-free vanilla

¼ cup gluten-free, casein-free soy milk

1½ cups frozen mixed berries

1. Preheat oven to 350°F.

2. Oil a standard muffin pan.

3. In a small bowl, combine flour, xanthan gum, 1 teaspoon baking powder and salt.

4. In a separate bowl, combine applesauce and ½ teaspoon baking powder.

5. Add flaxseed meal, melted margarine, brown sugar, vanilla, and soy milk to applesauce mixture.

6. Mix dry ingredients into wet, one half at a time.

7. Stir in berries. (If using frozen berries, there is no need to thaw them beforehand.)

8. Spoon batter into muffin pan.

9. Bake 25–30 minutes or until a toothpick inserted into the center of a muffin comes out clean.

MAKES 12 MUFFINS

Calories: 182 | Fat: 5 g | Protein: 2 g | Fiber: 3 g

Without Dairy, Where Can You Get Calcium?

An easy way to ensure that your child gets calcium throughout the day is to use a vitamin-fortified milk alternative. Many soy, rice, and nut drinks are enriched with calcium and vitamin D, which facilitates the body's absorption of calcium. Many brands of soy yogurt and fruit juice are also available with added vitamins.

PB & J Muffins

These muffins are a great alternative to peanut butter and jelly sandwiches. When gluten-free bread doesn't pack well, these muffins make a great stand-in.

INGREDIENTS

2 cups gluten-free oat flour

1½ teaspoons baking powder, divided

½ teaspoon salt

½ cup applesauce

½ cup flaxseed meal

¾ cup packed light brown sugar

1 teaspoon gluten-free vanilla

½ cup gluten-free, casein-free soy milk

¾ cup peanut butter (or sunflower-seed or almond butter)

1½ cups chopped raspberries

1. Preheat oven to 350°F.

2. Oil a standard muffin pan.

3. In a medium bowl, combine oat flour, 1 teaspoon baking powder, and salt.

4. In a separate bowl, combine applesauce with ½ teaspoon baking powder.

5. Add flaxseed meal, brown sugar, vanilla, soy milk, and peanut butter.

6. Mix dry ingredients into wet, one half at a time.

7. Mix in raspberries.

8. Spoon batter into oiled muffin pan.

9. Bake 25–30 minutes or until a toothpick inserted into the center of a muffin comes out clean.

MAKES 12 MUFFINS

Calories: 324 | Fat: 12 g | Protein: 10 g | Fiber: 4 g

Spicy Pumpkin Muffins

These muffins are so delicious that if you top them with Vanilla Frosting (page 215) they can pass as cupcakes.

INGREDIENTS

2½ cups gluten-free all-purpose flour

1 teaspoon xanthan gum

2¼ teaspoons baking powder, divided

¾ teaspoon salt

1½ teaspoons cinnamon

½ teaspoon nutmeg

¾ cup applesauce

¼ cup canola oil

1 cup packed dark brown sugar

1 teaspoon gluten-free vanilla

1 (15-ounce) can solid-packed pumpkin

½ cup dried cherries

Fresh Muffins Taste Best

Gluten-free muffins are slightly more fragile than traditional muffins. They taste best fresh from the oven, but will keep for up to three days in a sealed container. They can also be frozen for up to two months. To best enjoy muffins after the first day, warm them before serving.

1. Preheat oven to 350°F.

2. Oil a standard muffin pan.

3. In a large bowl, combine flour, xanthan gum, 1½ teaspoons baking powder, salt, cinnamon, and nutmeg.

4. In a separate bowl, combine applesauce and ¾ teaspoon baking powder.

5. Add oil, brown sugar, vanilla, and pumpkin to applesauce mixture. Stir until smooth.

6. Mix dry ingredients into wet, one half at a time.

7. Stir dried cherries into batter.

8. Spoon batter into oiled muffin pan.

9. Bake 18–23 minutes or until a toothpick inserted into the center of a muffin comes out clean.

MAKES 12 MUFFINS

Calories: 215 | Fat: 6 g | Protein: 3 g | Fiber: 4 g

Pie Crust

This is a really great, basic pie crust.
If you want a sweeter pie crust, increase the sugar.

INGREDIENTS

½ cup (4 ounces) gluten-free, casein-free soy cream cheese

½ cup (4 ounces) gluten-free, casein-free margarine

½ cup gluten-free all-purpose flour

¼ teaspoon xanthan gum

¼ teaspoon salt

¾ teaspoon sugar

1. Preheat oven to 350°F.

2. Mix together soy cream cheese and margarine until smooth and creamy.

3. Mix in remaining ingredients.

4. Shape dough into a disk. Press into pie pan.

5. Prick crust with a fork.

6. Bake for 10 minutes. Fill with desired filling and bake according to pie recipe.

MAKES 1 PIE CRUST

Calories: 151 | Fat: 12 g | Protein: 1 g | Fiber: 1 g

CHAPTER 5

Soup's On!

Gluten-Free Noodle Soup

Gluten-free noodles are available in a variety of shapes.
For this soup, choose a smaller-size variety.

INGREDIENTS

Approximately 10 cups water (enough to cover chicken)

1 large broiler-fryer chicken

3–4 celery stalks, chopped

4–6 carrots, chopped

1 large onion

1–2 tomatoes

Salt and pepper

2 bay leaves

2 teaspoons gluten-free chicken bouillon

1½ cups cooked gluten-free noodles (small size)

1. Bring water to a boil. Add chicken and return to a boil.

2. Once boiling, reduce heat immediately. Skim top of soup.

3. Add remaining ingredients and simmer for 1½ hours.

4. Remove chicken and set aside. Remove all vegetables and discard bay leaf.

5. Strain soup and allow to cool. Skim off hardened fat.

6. Reheat soup and add cooked noodles.

YIELDS 8 CUPS

Calories: 308 | Fat: 22 g | Protein: 12 g | Fiber: 3 g

Lentil Soup

*Divide this soup and freeze in small portions
to have meals ready for the future.*

INGREDIENTS

1 tablespoon olive oil

1 garlic clove

¾ cup diced onion

4 cups water

1 gluten-free, casein-free bouillon
   cube (vegetable, chicken, or
   beef)

1 cup diced carrots

½ cup diced celery

½ cup lentils

2 cups diced tomatoes with liquid

1. In a large stock pot, heat olive oil over medium-high flame.

2. Sauté garlic and onion for five minutes.

3. Add water, bouillon cube, carrots, and celery.

4. Rinse and pick over lentils, and add to pot.

5. Add tomatoes.

6. Cover and simmer for 45 minutes.

MAKES 6 CUPS

Calories: 115 | Fat: 3 g | Protein: 6 g | Fiber: 7 g

Taco Soup

This is a great meal on a cold night! It is a chili with a taco twist. Serve this with some baked or fried corn tortilla strips on top for a nice crunch to the soup.

INGREDIENTS

2 pounds 95 percent lean ground beef, ground turkey, or shredded chicken

1 teaspoon olive oil

1 large onion

2 (14-ounce) cans diced tomatoes with chilis, not drained

1 (14-ounce) can red kidney beans, not drained

1 (10-ounce) bag of frozen corn

1 Taco Seasoning Mixture (page 132)

1. In a large sauté pan, brown beef or turkey and drain. If you are using chicken, boil the chicken until cooked, remove from water, and shred.

2. In a large stock pot, heat olive oil over medium-high flame.

3. Sauté onion for five minutes, until clear.

4. Add meat, tomatoes, kidney beans, frozen corn, and Taco Seasoning Mixture.

5. Mix together well.

6. Heat over medium heat until heated through.

MAKES 8 CUPS

Calories: 265 | Fat: 7 g | Protein: 28 g | Fiber: 6 g

Chicken Noodle Soup

Boiling chicken in chicken noodle soup makes it very tender, so that children who have trouble with firmer textures might have an easier time with this dish.

INGREDIENTS

1 pound boneless chicken breasts cut into ¼-inch pieces

½ red onion, diced

2 celery ribs, sliced

1 medium carrot, sliced

¼ red bell pepper, diced

3 garlic cloves, minced

2 tablespoons gluten-free, casein-free margarine

2 tablespoons olive or canola oil

1 teaspoon dried basil

½ teaspoon dried oregano

⅛ teaspoon pepper

3 (14½-ounce) cans gluten-free, casein-free chicken broth

1 (14½-ounce) can diced tomatoes, undrained

½ summer squash or zucchini, sliced

4 cups gluten-free rotini, cooked according to package directions

5 ounces fresh spinach, chopped

1. In a large saucepan, sauté the chicken, onion, celery, carrots, red pepper, and garlic in margarine and oil for 5 minutes.

2. Stir in the basil, oregano, and pepper until blended.

3. Slowly add organic chicken broth, tomatoes, and zucchini or squash.

4. Bring to a boil. Reduce heat; cover and simmer for 1 hour.

5. Return to a boil; stir in the pasta and spinach.

6. Reduce heat; simmer, uncovered, for 5–10 minutes or until spinach is tender.

MAKES 8 CUPS

Calories: 141 | Fat: 4 g | Protein: 7 g | Fiber: 5 g

Cream of Potato Soup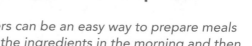

Crock-pots or slow cookers can be an easy way to prepare meals for your family. Assemble the ingredients in the morning and then forget about it until it's time for dinner!

INGREDIENTS

6 potatoes, peeled and cubed

2 onions, chopped

1 carrot, sliced

1 stalk celery, sliced

4 gluten-free, casein-free bouillon cubes (vegetable, chicken, or beef)

1 tablespoon parsley flakes

5 cups water

⅓ cup gluten-free, casein-free margarine

1½ cups gluten-free, casein-free soy milk

1. Put all ingredients except soy milk into a slow cooker.

2. Cover and cook on low for 10–12 hours or on high for 3–4 hours.

3. Stir in soy milk in last hour.

4. Control consistency in the soup by adding instant gluten-free mashed potatoes, if needed.

YIELDS 6 SERVINGS

Calories: 342 | Fat: 2 g | Protein: 9 g | Fiber: 10 g

A Soup a Day . . .

Soups are a fantastic base for children's menus. It is easy to incorporate many different vegetables in soups that your child may not venture to taste on his or her own.

Creamy Cauliflower Soup

For added texture, remove ⅓ of the soup before pureeing.
After soup is pureed, return to pot and combine with reserved soup.

INGREDIENTS

1 medium cauliflower

½ onion

1 tablespoon olive oil

3 medium potatoes

4 cups gluten-free, casein-free
   vegetable broth

2 tablespoons nutritional yeast

½ teaspoon white pepper

½ teaspoon sea salt

1 bay leaf

1 cup gluten-free, casein-free
   plain soy yogurt

The White "Green" Vegetable

The saying "eat your green vegetables" should have the amendment—"and cauliflower." This late-season nutritional powerhouse is a cruciferous vegetable; it's in the same family as broccoli, cabbage, and kale. It has high levels of vitamin C and significant amounts of vitamin B6, folate, and dietary fiber.

1. Peel and dice potatoes.

2. Chop cauliflower.

3. In a large stock pot, sauté onion in olive oil.

4. Add remaining ingredients, bring to a boil.

5. Reduce heat to a simmer.

6. Simmer approximately 30 minutes until potatoes and cauliflower are tender.

7. Remove bay leaf.

8. Puree soup in blender until smooth.

MAKES 6 CUPS

Calories: 229 | Fat: 3 g | Protein: 7 g | Fiber: 7 g

Minestrone Soup

This hearty, delicious soup is great for a crowd! Use this for winter gatherings or potluck dinners. Rice stands in for pasta in this healthy dish.

INGREDIENTS

1 red onion, chopped

3 cloves garlic, minced

1 tablespoon olive oil

6 cups gluten-free, casein-free stock (vegetable, chicken, or beef)

2 (14½-ounce) cans stewed tomatoes with Italian seasoning

1 large potato, cubed

2 stalks celery, chopped

2 carrots, chopped

¼ large head cabbage, finely chopped

1 cup uncooked brown rice

½ tablespoon thyme

½ tablespoon oregano

2 tablespoons chopped fresh basil

1 (15-ounce) can cannellini beans

2 cups fresh corn kernels

1 large zucchini, sliced

¼ cup parsley, chopped

Vegan Parmesan cheese (optional)

Salt and pepper to taste

1. In a large soup pot, sauté onions and garlic in 1 tablespoon olive oil until clear.

2. Add in the vegetable stock, undrained tomatoes, potato, celery, carrot, cabbage, rice, thyme, oregano, and basil.

3. Bring to a boil and reduce heat. Simmer for about 15 minutes.

4. Stir in the beans, corn, zucchini, and parsley.

5. Simmer for 20–30 more minutes until the vegetables are tender.

6. Season with salt and pepper. Sprinkle with vegan Parmesan cheese to serve.

YIELDS 10 CUPS

Calories: 192 | Fat: 3 g | Protein: 8 g | Fiber: 7 g

Beaneaters!

Cannellini beans are so popular in the Tuscany region in Italy that the Tuscan people have been nicknamed *mangiafagiole*, which means beaneaters. These beans can be used in place of great northern beans or navy beans in most recipes. The nutritional benefits are that they are high in fiber, folate, iron, and magnesium.

Split Pea Soup

This protein-rich soup is also a good source of vitamin A, vitamin C, potassium, and dietary fiber.

INGREDIENTS

1 cup split peas

1 medium onion

1 medium carrot

1 medium baking potato

1 teaspoon olive oil

3 cups gluten-free, casein-free broth (vegetable, chicken, or beef)

¼ teaspoon dried summer savory

⅛ teaspoon cumin

1 bay leaf

Different Tastes and Textures

If your child has problems with food texture, throw away traditional ideas of food combinations. Culture largely dictates what foods "go together." Your child might think that other combinations are more appealing. For example, try adding chopped fruit to mashed potatoes for a vitamin-rich comfort food or serving cooled Split Pea Soup as a dip for pita chips.

1. Pick over split peas and remove any debris. Rinse, drain, and set aside.

2. Finely chop onion, carrot, and potato.

3. In a stock-pot, heat olive oil over medium-high heat.

4. Add vegetables and sauté until soft, approximately 3 minutes.

5. Add remaining ingredients. Stir.

6. Simmer uncovered 40 minutes, or until split peas are very soft.

7. Remove bay leaf.

8. Add more vegetable broth for a thinner soup, if desired.

MAKES 6 CUPS

Calories: 388 | Fat: 2 g | Protein: 25 g | Fiber: 26 g

Creamy Corn Chowder

For a smooth soup, blend all of it, rather than reserving some to mix in.

INGREDIENTS

4 baking potatoes

1 onion

2 large, peeled carrots

1 green bell pepper

4 cups corn (or 1 pound frozen)

6 cups water

2 gluten-free, casein-free bouillon cubes (vegetable, chicken, or beef)

1 cup gluten-free, casein-free soy milk

Fresh-ground pepper

1. Coarsely chop all vegetables, except corn.

2. Combine all ingredients, except soy milk and pepper, in a large stock pot.

3. Bring to a boil.

4. Reduce heat, simmer ½ hour or until vegetables are tender.

5. Remove 5 cups of soup from pot and blend until smooth in a blender. Return blended soup to pot.

6. Mix in soy milk and pepper to taste; heat before serving.

MAKES 7 CUPS

Calories: 214 | Fat: 1 g | Protein: 8 g | Fiber: 7 g

Turkey Chili

If this chili is not spicy enough for the adults, add extra chili powder and green chilis or serrano peppers to an adult portion and heat through.

INGREDIENTS

2 tablespoons canola oil

1 red onion, chopped

1 clove garlic, minced

1 pound ground turkey breast

1 pound butternut squash, peeled, seeded and cut into 1-inch cubes

½ cup gluten-free, casein-free chicken broth

2 (14½-ounce) cans petite diced tomatoes

1 (15-ounce) can black beans with liquid

1 (15½-ounce) can white hominy, drained

1 (8-ounce) can tomato sauce

2 teaspoons chili powder

1 tablespoon ground cumin

⅛ teaspoon cinnamon

8 ounces gluten-free, casein-free plain soy yogurt

1. In a large pot, heat the canola oil over medium heat. Add onion and garlic; cook and stir for 3 minutes until clear, add turkey. Stir until crumbly and no longer pink.

2. Add the butternut squash, chicken broth, tomatoes, black beans, hominy, and tomato sauce; season with chili powder, cumin, and cinnamon.

3. Bring to a simmer, then reduce heat to medium-low, cover, and simmer until the squash is tender, about 20 minutes.

4. Top each bowl with 1–2 tablespoons of yogurt to serve.

YIELDS 12 CUPS

Calories: 195 | Fat: 6 g | Protein: 11 g | Fiber: 5 g

Vegetable Rice Soup

This soup cooks up pretty thick.
If you want a thinner soup, add some vegetable or chicken broth.

INGREDIENTS

1 carrot

1 celery stalk

1 potato

½ small onion

1 small sweet potato

1 cup chopped spinach

1 cup brown rice

8 cups water

1 (15-ounce) can diced tomatoes

½ teaspoon dried oregano

½ teaspoon dried basil

½ teaspoon dried thyme

1. Finely chop all vegetables.

2. Combine all ingredients in a large stock pot.

3. Bring to a boil.

4. Reduce heat, cover, and simmer for 45 minutes or until rice is soft.

MAKES 10 CUPS

Calories: 124 | Fat: 1 g | Protein: 4 g | Fiber: 3 g

Flexible Foods

There is almost nothing as frustrating as starting a recipe, confident that you have all of the ingredients on hand, and then discovering that you're missing a key component of your dish. Not to worry, because there is often a fine substitute right at hand. If you don't have brown rice, substitute white rice or quinoa. If you don't have strawberries, try blueberries or peaches instead. One green usually fills in nicely for another in cooked dishes, so if you have collard greens, go ahead and use them instead of spinach.

White Chili 👨‍🍳

*White chili is called white because
most of the ingredients are white in color.*

INGREDIENTS

1 medium onion, chopped

2 cloves garlic, minced

1 tablespoon canola oil

2 organic cooked chicken breasts, cubed

1 (12-ounce) can of white corn, drained

1 (15-ounce) can cannellini beans, drained

1 (15-ounce) can garbanzo beans, drained

1 (4-ounce) can green chilis

2 (14½-ounce) cans gluten-free, casein-free chicken broth

6 ounces shredded gluten-free, casein-free soy Monterey jack cheese

1. In large stock pot, sauté onion and garlic in oil until tender.

2. Add next 6 ingredients to pot and simmer for 20–30 minutes or until heated through and beans are tender.

3. Top each serving with soy cheese.

YIELDS 8 CUPS

Calories: 247 | Fat: 5 g | Protein: 16 g | Fiber: 7 g

One-Color Meals!

This is an all white chili, meaning all the ingredients that go into it are the color white. Try this as a way to excite your child about a meal; serve an "all-same-color" meal every once in a while. For instance, an orange meal might be orange slices, mashed sweet potatoes, and macaroni and cheese with carrot coins.

Garlic Broth with Tomatoes and Spinach

To make a heartier soup, add cooked rice or beans.

INGREDIENTS

3 tablespoons minced garlic

¼ teaspoon dried thyme

½ teaspoon paprika

2 tablespoons olive oil

6 cups vegetable broth

1 bunch fresh spinach

1½ cups diced tomato

Salt and pepper to taste

Boost Your Flavor with Broth!

Next time you're cooking rice, quinoa, or gluten-free pasta, consider using broth as the liquid instead of water. You will get a more flavorful dish to serve either on its own or to use in a recipe.

1. Over medium heat, sauté garlic, thyme, and paprika in olive oil until the garlic is fragrant, but not browned.

2. Bring broth to a boil, add garlic mixture to the boil and reduce heat to simmer.

3. Clean spinach, and chop damp leaves.

4. Wilt spinach over medium heat.

5. Add spinach and diced tomatoes to simmering broth.

6. Add salt and pepper to taste.

MAKES 8 CUPS

Calories: 112 | Fat: 7 g | Protein: 3 g | Fiber: 3 g

CHAPTER 6

What's for Breakfast

Banana Soy Yogurt Milkshake

Agave nectar or honey can be used to sweeten this to your taste. Use different flavored yogurts to make different flavored organic milkshakes. Blending up crushed ice in the organic milkshake creates a thicker shake.

INGREDIENTS

1 banana

1 tablespoon lemon juice

8 ounces gluten-free, casein-free vanilla soy yogurt

1 cup gluten-free, casein-free soy milk

1 tablespoon ground flaxseeds

Combine all ingredients in a blender until smooth.

YIELDS 2 CUPS

Calories: 430 | Fat: 8 g | Protein: 15 g | Fiber: 8 g

Blueberry and Banana Soy Yogurt with Crispy Rice

Yogurt gets a nutrition and texture boost with fresh banana and crispy rice.

INGREDIENTS

½ ripe banana

8 ounces gluten-free, casein-free blueberry soy yogurt

¼ cup gluten-free crispy rice cereal

1. Mash banana with a fork.

2. Combine with blueberry yogurt.

3. Stir in crispy rice cereal.

MAKES 2 CUPS

Calories: 272 | Fat: 4 g | Protein: 10 g | Fiber: 3 g

The Breakfast Challenge

Gluten-free rice- and corn-based cereals can be early morning heroes for anyone following a gluten-free diet. The key is to double-check that the cereal is actually gluten-free. Some rice or corn-based cereals use barley malt as a sweetener, making them not a good option on a gluten-free/casein-free diet.

Granola

Making your own granola can open up cereal options for your child. Check with your doctor to make sure gluten-free oats are okay for your child.

INGREDIENTS

2 cups gluten-free oats

⅓ cup chopped pecans

¼ cup chopped almonds

¼ cup apple juice

¼ cup pure maple syrup

2 tablespoons canola oil

1 teaspoon cinnamon

½ cup dried apple pieces

Mix It Up!

Using different dried fruits in your granola can really change the flavor. Try dried cherries, raisins, or even dried blueberries in your granola. Changing nuts can also shake up the flavor. Cashews, walnuts, or even sunflower and pumpkin seeds can all make a yummy granola.

1. Preheat oven to 350°F.

2. Oil a cookie sheet.

3. In a large bowl, combine oats, nuts, apple juice, maple syrup, oil, and cinnamon.

4. Spread mixture on cookie sheet.

5. Bake 15–20 minutes or until golden brown.

6. When cool, combine with dried apples.

MAKES 10 SERVINGS

Calories: 153 | Fat: 8 g | Protein: 3 g | Fiber: 2 g

Blueberry Syrup for Waffles

Serve this yummy syrup over gluten-free waffles.

INGREDIENTS

2 cups blueberries

⅓ cup apple juice concentrate

1 tablespoon cornstarch

2 tablespoons cold water

Blueberries on Ice

Freezing blueberries at home is a great way to make the taste of summer last all year. Wash the blueberries, dry them, and pick out any damaged berries. Then, spread the berries out on a cookie sheet and freeze. Once frozen solid, transfer the berries to a freezer-safe container, where they can be enjoyed for up to one year.

1. In a small saucepan, combine blueberries and apple juice concentrate.

2. Simmer 10 minutes.

3. While the fruit is simmering, combine cornstarch and water in a small bowl.

4. Add cornstarch mixture to blueberries.

5. Simmer and stir continuously, until thickened.

MAKES 2 CUPS

Per cup:
Calories: 160 | Fat: 0.5 g | Protein: 1.5 g | Fiber: 7 g

Breakfast Pizza

If you're going to wait to serve this, dip the bananas in orange, lemon, or lime juice to prevent browning. Bananas and apples turn brown because an enzyme in them reacts with oxygen. Acidic juices stop this browning!

INGREDIENTS

4 corn tortillas

½ teaspoon gluten-free, casein-free margarine

1 teaspoon table sugar

⅛ teaspoon cinnamon

⅓ cup gluten-free, casein-free soy cream cheese

2 teaspoons honey

¼ cup organic blueberries

¼ cup organic strawberries, sliced

½ cup organic blackberries

¼ cup bananas

¼ cup kiwi, diced

1. Preheat oven to 400°F.

2. Place corn tortillas on an ungreased cookie sheet.

3. Spread margarine evenly over each tortilla.

4. Separately, combine table sugar and cinnamon. Sprinkle over the top of each tortilla.

5. Bake tortillas for 3–4 minutes or until edges begin to brown. Remove from oven.

6. To make topping, beat cream cheese with honey until well mixed.

7. Spread over the tortillas forming a base for the fruit toppings.

8. Arrange fruit on top of tortillas. Cut into pizza slices and serve.

YIELDS 4 PIZZAS

Calories: 255 | Fat: 9 g | Protein: 4 g | Fiber: 4 g

Cantaloupe Papaya Smoothie

This smoothie is a vibrant orange color.
It pleases the eyes as well as the taste buds.

INGREDIENTS

1 cup frozen cantaloupe chunks

½ cup frozen papaya chunks

½ cup orange juice

1 cup gluten-free, casein-free soy milk

Combine all ingredients in a blender. Blend until smooth.

MAKES 2¼ CUPS

Calories: 121 | Fat: 1 g | Protein: 3 g | Fiber: 3 g

Fresh Fruit Slush

This tangy mixture can be used as a light dip for fruit or as a dressing to drizzle over fresh fruit. Frozen mangos and strawberries can also be used together as an alternative to peaches.

INGREDIENTS

1 (10-ounce) package frozen unsweetened peach slices, thawed

1 (10-ounce) package frozen unsweetened sliced strawberries, thawed

2 tablespoons light agave nectar

1 tablespoon lemon juice

1 teaspoon lime juice

¼ teaspoon gluten-free vanilla

1. Combine all ingredients in a food processor.

2. Process until smooth.

YIELDS 3 CUPS

Per cup:
Calories: 222 | Fat: 0 g | Protein: 1 g | Fiber: 4 g

Fruit Kabobs 👨‍🍳

Using plastic straws instead of sharp toothpicks or skewers makes this a safer treat to enjoy.

INGREDIENTS

¼ cup cantaloupe cubes

¼ cup honeydew cubes

¼ cup pineapple cubes

¼ cup peach cubes

Small plastic straws (or drink stirrers)

1. Cut each fruit into 1-inch cubes.

2. Thread cubes onto the straw, alternating fruits.

MAKES 4 KABOBS

Calories: 16 | Fat: 0 g | Protein: 0 g | Fiber: 0 g

Have Fun with Food!

Creating playful presentations can be fun for parents and children alike. Making smiley-face pancakes using artfully arranged blueberries or creating a flower out of fruit salad can make meal-time a happy time for everyone.

Mixed Fruit and Soy Yogurt Smoothie

Feel free to substitute other fruits,
such as honeydew, strawberries, or bananas.

INGREDIENTS

1 cup frozen cantaloupe chunks

1 cup frozen pineapple pieces

1 cup frozen blueberries

1 cup gluten-free, casein-free
   vanilla soy yogurt

1 cup gluten-free, casein-free soy
   milk

1 cup apple juice

1. Combine all ingredients in a
   blender.

2. Blend until smooth.

MAKES 5 CUPS

Calories: 210 | Fat: 1 g | Protein: 3 g | Fiber: 2 g

Enriched Nondairy Milk Alternatives

When switching to a casein-free diet, there are a number of milk alternatives to consider. Look for vitamin-enriched milk alternatives that include calcium and vitamin D. High-quality options include soy, rice, oat, or even hemp milk. For children who are avoiding nuts due to possible food allergy, nut milks should be avoided.

Oatmeal with Cinnamon Apples

If your doctor has determined that it would be best to avoid oats, other gluten-free hot cereals would work really well in place of the oats.

INGREDIENTS

½ cup water

½ cup apple juice

1 Golden Delicious apple, cored and chopped

⅔ cup gluten-free rolled oats

1 teaspoon ground cinnamon

1–2 tablespoons agave nectar light

1 cup gluten-free, casein-free soy milk

Why a Frozen Banana?

Using a frozen banana helps improve the texture of this drink and makes it more smoothie-like. To make a frozen banana, just peel a ripe banana, place it in a Zip-loc bag, and freeze overnight.

1. In a small saucepan, combine water, apple juice, and apple pieces. Bring to a boil.

2. Once boiling, stir in rolled oats and cinnamon. Return to a boil.

3. Reduce heat down to low and simmer to desired thickness, 3–5 minutes.

4. Add agave nectar to reach desired sweetness.

5. Pour soy milk over servings and serve.

YIELDS 2 CUPS

Calories: 300 | Fat: 3 g | Protein: 6 g | Fiber: 7 g

Orange Pineapple Smoothie

The combination of orange and pineapple is sure to bring a little sun (not to mention lots of vitamin C) into even the gloomiest day.

INGREDIENTS

1 cup frozen pineapple chunks

½ frozen banana

¾ cup orange juice

¾ cup gluten-free, casein-free soy milk

Combine all ingredients in a blender. Blend until smooth.

MAKES 2¼ CUPS

Calories: 147 | Fat: 1 g | Protein: 3 g | Fiber: 3 g

Peach Raspberry Compote

*Serve this compote with a hot cereal like grits
or on top of gluten-free frozen waffles.*

INGREDIENTS

1 cup chopped peaches

1 cup raspberries

2 tablespoons apple juice
concentrate

Simmer all ingredients until fruit starts
to soften and break down,
approximately 10 minutes.

MAKES 2 CUPS

Calories: 170 | Fat: 1 g | Protein: 3 g | Fiber: 10 g

What a Peach!

The peach, a sweet vitamin-rich
summer fruit, is so delightful
that Americans use its name to
conjure up all kinds of positive
images. From the complimen-
tary, "She's a peach," to the
upbeat, "I'm feeling peachy,"
the peach has become a syn-
onym for sweetness. Although
the nectarine is a smooth-
skinned variety of peach, you
just don't hear anyone saying,
"You're such a nectarine!"

Pink Soy Milk

Why use mixes that are loaded with sugar and artificial colors and flavors to give milk a fun boost when the natural alternative is so easy?

INGREDIENTS

2 cups gluten-free, casein-free
   soy milk

¼ cup chopped strawberries

Combine all ingredients in a blender. Blend until smooth.

MAKES 2 CUPS

Calories: 106 | Fat: 2 g | Protein: 4 g | Fiber: 2 g

Boost the Vitamins While Boosting Flavor!

Blending strawberries, blueberries, peaches, or pineapple with a nondairy milk alternative can make getting your calcium a treat. Fresh or frozen fruits add a burst of color, sweetness, and vitamins.

Strawberry Applesauce

Strawberries provide a pretty and vitamin-rich addition to traditional applesauce.

INGREDIENTS

1 cup apples, peeled and diced

1 cup strawberries, cut

¼ cup organic apple juice

I Like to Eat, Eat, Eat . . . Apples and Carrots!

Apples are a popular food to mix other foods with. Many fruits combined with apples will create wonderful "sauces." Try unique combinations of fruits and vegetables. For example, create a mixed berry applesauce using blackberries and blueberries. Whip up an orange applesauce, or even try a carrot applesauce!

1. In a medium saucepan, combine all ingredients.

2. Cover and simmer for about 10–15 minutes, until fruit is tender.

3. Mash with potato masher or puree in blender to desired consistency.

YIELDS 2 CUPS

Calories: 143 | Fat: 1 g | Protein: 1 g | Fiber: 6 g

Strawberry Banana Soy Yogurt

*Add some texture to this smooth breakfast
by mixing in dried fruit or cereal.*

INGREDIENTS

1 cup gluten-free, casein-free
   vanilla soy yogurt

½ cup sliced strawberries

½ sliced banana

½ teaspoon cinnamon

Combine all ingredients in a bowl and
mix well with a spoon.

YIELDS 2 CUPS

Calories: 134 | Fat: 2 g | Protein: 5 g | Fiber: 2 g

Strawberry Blueberry Banana Smoothie

This smoothie has a delightful purple hue.

INGREDIENTS

½ cup frozen strawberries

½ cup frozen blueberries

½ frozen banana

½ cup apple juice

1 cup gluten-free, casein-free soy milk

Combine all ingredients in a blender. Blend until smooth.

MAKES 2¼ CUPS

Calories: 138 | Fat: 1 g | Protein: 3 g | Fiber: 3 g

Strawberry Topping

This very simple sauce is a tasty topping
for sorbet, waffles, or hot cereal.

INGREDIENTS

1 cup chopped strawberries

¼ cup water

1. In a small saucepan, combine strawberries and water.

2. Cook over medium heat, breaking up strawberries with the back of a spoon as they cook.

3. Serve warm or at room temperature.

MAKES 1 CUP

Calories: 49 | Fat: 0 g | Protein: 1 g | Fiber: 3 g

Sunflower-Seed Butter and Banana Smoothie

This smoothie provides protein, calcium, and potassium in the guise of a treat.

INGREDIENTS

1½ frozen bananas

⅓ cup sunflower-seed butter

⅓ cup apple juice

2 cups gluten-free, casein-free soy milk

2 teaspoons agave nectar

1. Combine all ingredients in a blender.

2. Blend until smooth.

MAKES 4 CUPS

Calories: 200 | Fat: 11 g | Protein: 6 g | Fiber: 1 g

Sunflower Seeds Not Just for the Birds

Sunflower seeds, the mainstay of many wild bird feeders and baseball pitchers, are a great source of nutrition for your family. They are great sources of vitamin E and folate, plus a host of minerals. They are also a good source of protein and good fats. So, grind some up into sunflower-seed butter and add them to your recipes for a creamy, health-improving boost.

Tofu Scramble

To make this quick entree even more convenient,
use thawed frozen chopped spinach.

INGREDIENTS

1 tablespoon olive oil

1 minced garlic clove

½ cup minced onion

1 cup chopped spinach

15 ounces extra-firm tofu

1 tablespoon gluten-free, casein-
free soy sauce

1. In a large skillet or sauté pan, heat olive oil over medium-high heat.

2. Sauté garlic and onion until soft, golden, and fragrant.

3. Add spinach, and sauté until wilted.

4. Crumble tofu and add to skillet.

5. Add soy sauce.

6. Cook over medium-high heat until heated through, approximately 7 minutes.

YIELDS 3 SERVINGS (¾ CUP PER SERVING)

Calories: 195 | Fat: 12 g | Protein: 15 g | Fiber: 3 g

Tropical Fruit Smoothie

This summery treat is loaded with vitamins A and C.

INGREDIENTS

½ cup frozen pineapple chunks

½ cup frozen mango chunks

½ cup frozen strawberries

1 cup gluten-free, casein-free soy milk

½ cup orange juice

Combine all ingredients in a blender. Blend until smooth.

YIELDS 2 SERVINGS (1¼ CUP PER SERVINGS)

Calories: 137 | Fat: 1 g | Protein: 3 g | Fiber: 3 g

Smoothie Tricks and Tips

Not all children are comfortable with the feeling of cold smoothie on their lips. Don't give up after the first attempt. Straws can be helpful for some children. Another thing to try is to blend a thicker smoothie and serve it with a spoon.

Good Morning Pancakes

These yummy pancakes are great with syrup, jam, or cut-up fruit.

INGREDIENTS

2 cups gluten-free all-purpose flour

½ teaspoon xanthan gum

½ cup cornmeal

½ cup sugar

2½ teaspoons baking powder, divided

2 teaspoons baking soda

¼ teaspoon salt

½ cup applesauce

2¼ cups gluten-free, casein-free soy milk

¼ cup melted gluten-free, casein-free margarine

1 teaspoon gluten-free vanilla

Blueberry Pancakes

To dress up pancakes, add 1 cup blueberries to the batter before cooking. Blueberry pancakes are a great Sunday morning treat.

1. In a medium bowl, using a whisk, mix together flour, xanthan gum, cornmeal, sugar, 2 teaspoons of baking powder, baking soda, and salt.

2. In a large bowl, combine applesauce with ½ teaspoon baking powder.

3. Add soy milk, one half of the melted margarine, and the vanilla to the applesauce mixture.

4. Mix the dry ingredients into the wet until just combined.

5. Brush a skillet or griddle with melted margarine.

6. Heat until a drop of water "dances" on the surface of the pan.

7. Pour approximately ¼ cup of batter onto hot pan.

8. When the edge of the pancake is golden brown, turn it and cook through on the other side. Continue with all of the batter.

MAKES 12 PANCAKES

Calories: 197 | Fat: 5 g | Protein: 3 g | Fiber: 6 g

Crispy Potato Pancakes

This is basically a good, old kosher recipe. It is marvelous with applesauce, gluten-free, casein-free sour cream, or both. For brunch, it's excellent with eggs on the side.

INGREDIENTS

4 Idaho potatoes, peeled and coarsely grated

2 mild onions, chopped fine

2 eggs, well beaten

½ cup potato flour

Salt and pepper to taste

2 cups cooking oil (such as canola)

Applesauce, fruit preserves, salsa, or chutney to garnish

1. Mix the grated potatoes, onions, and eggs in a bowl. Sprinkle with potato flour, salt, and pepper.

2. Heat the oil to 350°F and spoon in the potato cakes, pressing down to make a patty.

3. Fry until golden, about 5 minutes per side. Drain, keep warm, and serve with garnish of choice.

MAKES ABOUT 10 PANCAKES

Calories: 317 | Fat: 24 g | Protein: 4 g | Fiber: 2 g

The Origins of Potato Pancakes

During the long winters in northern and eastern Europe, when fresh fruits and vegetables were not available, winter storage of carrots, potatoes, beets, Brussels sprouts, apples, and dried fruits was crucial to prevent scurvy, or ascorbic acid deficiency. As Mother Nature would have it, these vegetables are packed with vitamins and minerals. Potato pancakes with applesauce or fruit syrups became a staple in harsh climates.

Skillet Breakfast

Serve this skillet alone or topped with scrambled eggs or tofu.

INGREDIENTS

1 bell pepper, chopped

½ onion, chopped

6 button mushrooms, chopped

1 clove garlic, minced

3 tablespoons olive oil

3 medium white potatoes, cooked and diced

1 tomato, chopped

¼ cup grated gluten- and casein-free Cheddar cheese (optional)

1. Sauté pepper, onion, mushrooms, and garlic in olive oil until vegetables are tender.

2. Add potatoes and cook until potatoes are browned.

3. Add tomato and cook until mixture is heated through.

4. Top with cheese, if using.

SERVES 4

Calories: 373 | Fat: 13 g | Protein: 8 g | Fiber: 7 g

Fresh Mushroom Scramble

Simple and fresh ingredients come together to create this tasty and satisfying breakfast scramble.

INGREDIENTS

4 egg whites

8 whole eggs

2 tablespoons gluten-free, casein-free soy milk

Salt and pepper to taste

2 tablespoons gluten-free, casein-free Worcestershire sauce

2 small cloves garlic, crushed

2 teaspoons olive oil

12 fresh mushrooms, washed and stemmed

2 tablespoons chopped parsley

Freshly ground pepper to taste

1. Lightly whisk the egg whites in a large bowl. Add the whole eggs and soymilk and whisk until combined. Season lightly with salt and pepper.

2. Combine the Worcestershire sauce, garlic, and olive oil. Brush the mushrooms lightly with the Worcestershire sauce mixture, then grill or broil on medium heat for 5–7 minutes or until soft. Remove and keep warm.

3. Heat a nonstick frying pan and add the egg mixture, scraping the bottom gently with a flat plastic spatula to cook evenly. Cook until the egg is just set.

4. To serve, divide the scrambled eggs and mushrooms among four serving plates. Sprinkle the eggs with the chopped parsley and freshly ground pepper. Serve immediately.

SERVES 4

Calories: 196 | Fat: 12 g | Protein: 81 g | Fiber: 1 g

Spinach Omelet

The harmony of spinach and eggs makes this omelet not only pretty to look at but tasty and pleasing even to children.

INGREDIENTS

1 (10-ounce) package frozen chopped spinach, thawed and undrained

3 tablespoons gluten-free, casein-free chicken broth

1 clove garlic, crushed

⅛ to ¼ teaspoon pepper

¼ cup gluten-free, casein-free Parmesan cheese

10 eggs

2 tablespoons water

2 teaspoons gluten-free, casein-free margarine, divided

1. Combine spinach, broth, garlic, and pepper in a small saucepan; cover and simmer 20 minutes. Stir in Parmesan cheese; cook 1 minute or until cheese is melted, stirring constantly. Set aside.

2. Combine eggs and water; beat lightly. Coat a 10-inch omelet pan or heavy skillet with 1 teaspoon gluten-free, casein-free margarine. Place pan over medium heat until just hot enough to sizzle a drop of water.

3. Pour half of egg mixture into pan. As mixture starts to cook, gently lift edges of omelet with a spatula and tilt pan so uncooked portion flows underneath.

4. As mixture begins to set, spread half the spinach mixture over half the omelet. Loosen omelet with a spatula; fold in half and slide onto a warm serving platter.

5. Repeat procedure with remaining ingredients.

SERVES 6

Calories: 149 | Fat: 10 g | Protein: 12 g | Fiber: 1 g

Veggie Omelet

Colorful veggies add to the crunch and the appeal of this easy-to-prepare omelet. Not only are they gluten-free, casein-free ingredients, but they will also improve your family's overall health.

INGREDIENTS

½ cup thinly sliced mushrooms

¼ cup chopped green pepper

¼ cup chopped onion

1 tablespoon diced pimiento

3 eggs at room temperature, separated

2 tablespoons gluten-free, casein-free mayonnaise

¼ teaspoon salt

⅛ teaspoon pepper

Veggies and Gluten and Casein

You will be delighted to know that all fresh veggies and fruits are totally gluten free and casein free in their natural state. Grow your own, pick your own, or buy them fresh from the market—it doesn't matter as long as you cook with the freshest fruits and vegetables possible.

1. Combine mushrooms, green pepper, onion, and pimiento in a 1-quart casserole; cover loosely with heavy-duty plastic wrap and microwave on high for 3–3½ minutes or until vegetables are tender. Drain and set aside.

2. Beat egg whites until stiff peaks form. Combine egg yolks, mayonnaise, salt, and pepper; beat well. Gently fold egg whites into egg yolk mixture.

3. Coat a 9-inch glass pie plate or quiche pan with ½ teaspoon oil. Pour egg mixture into pie plate, spreading evenly. Microwave at medium (50 percent power) for 8–10½ minutes or until center is almost set, giving pie plate a half-turn after 5 minutes.

4. Spread vegetable mixture over half of omelet. Loosen omelet with spatula and fold in half. Slide the omelet onto a warm serving platter.

SERVES 2

Calories: 224 | Fat: 19 g | Protein: 10 g | Fiber: 1 g

Breakfast Potatoes

Potatoes are great for breakfast and these will wake up your taste buds. These quick and easy potatoes can even be made for a fast school-day breakfast!

INGREDIENTS

1 large baking potato

1½ tablespoons gluten-free, casein-free margarine

¼ teaspoon celery salt

¼ teaspoon paprika

⅛ teaspoon pepper

¼ cup finely chopped fresh parsley

1. Scrub potato and pat dry. Prick several times with a fork. Place potato on paper towel in microwave oven. Microwave on high 5–6 minutes, turning potato after 3 minutes.

2. Let potato stand 5 minutes to cool before checking for doneness. Cut potato into ¾-inch cubes and set aside.

3. Place margarine in a 1½-quart casserole. Microwave 30 seconds or until melted.

4. Stir celery salt, paprika, and pepper into margarine. Add potatoes and parsley. Toss all together.

5. Cover with casserole lid. Microwave on high for 2 minutes. Stir before serving.

SERVES 2

Calories: 219 | Fat: 9 g | Protein: 4 g | Fiber:7 g

CHAPTER 7

Sensational Salads and Slaws

Avocado Summer Salad

This recipe works nicely with many different summer fruits. Experiment with a variety of berries to provide different sources of vitamins, minerals, and antioxidants.

INGREDIENTS

2 ripe avocados

2 fresh nectarines

¾ cup strawberries, diced

¼ cup sweet onion, diced

3 tablespoons fresh-squeezed lime juice

Salt and ground black pepper to taste

1. Remove the pit from the avocados and slice into long strips.

2. Pit and dice the nectarines

3. Mix together the nectarines, strawberries, and onion in a bowl.

4. Toss the mixture until evenly coated.

5. Arrange the avocado slices on a plate.

6. Squeeze lime juice over the avocados to help maintain freshness.

7. Top avocados with the mixture of nectarines, strawberries, and onions.

8. Season with salt and pepper.

YIELDS 5 CUPS (4 SERVINGS)
Calories: 154 | Fat: 11 g | Protein: 2 g | Fiber: 6 g

Chicken Salad

Use this to stuff pea pods or celery as a fun snack for your children. You can also wrap it in a warmed corn tortilla for a sandwich.

INGREDIENTS

10 ounces canned white meat chicken, drained

2 tablespoons dried blueberries

¼ cup gluten-free, casein-free mayonnaise

Combine all ingredients.

YIELDS 10 OUNCES (4 SERVINGS)

Calories: 239 | Fat: 17 g | Protein: 16 g | Fiber: 1 g

Citrus Fruit Salad

Pair this recipe with the Cinnamon Soy Yogurt Fruit Dip, which is found on page 236. These two dishes together provide great sources of vitamin C and calcium. Jicama also provides a source of folic acid in this dish!

INGREDIENTS

2 oranges, peeled and sliced

1 cup pineapple, sliced

½ cup jicama, cut into matchsticks

1 cup blueberries

½ cup shredded coconut

1. Peel and slice oranges, pineapple, and jicama.

2. Combine slices with the blueberries.

3. Top with shredded coconut to taste.

YIELDS 4 SERVINGS

Calories: 136 | Fat: 4 g | Protein: 2 g | Fiber: 4 g

Citrusy Rice Salad

Keep the extra dressing in a separate container to redress any leftover salad.

INGREDIENTS

¼ cup green beans

¼ cup chopped orange pieces

¼ cup pineapple chunks

2 scallions

2 cups cooked short-grain brown rice

¼ cup orange juice

1 teaspoon agave nectar

¼ cup olive oil

1. Steam green beans until tender. Plunge into cold water to stop cooking process.

2. Cut fruit and beans into bite-size pieces.

3. Thinly slice white portion of scallion.

4. Combine rice, fruit, and vegetables.

5. In a jar with a tight-fitting lid, combine orange juice, agave nectar, and olive oil. Shake to combine.

6. Toss salad with dressing to taste.

MAKES 3 CUPS (6 SERVINGS)

Calories: 170 | Fat: 10 g | Protein: 2 g | Fiber: 2 g

Cucumber Tomato Salad

*This versatile salad can act as dip for corn chips,
or it can be used as a topping for fish or chicken.*

INGREDIENTS

4 hothouse tomatoes

1 cucumber

½ red onion

1 tablespoon minced garlic

2 tablespoons extra-virgin olive oil

3 tablespoons gluten-free, casein-
free red wine vinegar

Salt and pepper to taste

1. Dice tomatoes, cucumber, and onions.

2. In large mixing bowl, combine all ingredients.

3. Salt and pepper to taste.

YIELDS 4 CUPS

Calories: 109 | Fat: 10 g | Protein: 1 g | Fiber: 1 g

Picking an Olive Oil Is Confusing!

There are four descriptors that show the degree of processing in the olive oil. Extra-virgin olive oil means that this is the oil from the first pressing of the olives. Virgin olive oil is from the second pressing. Pure olive oil is then refined and filtered slightly. Extra-light oil has been highly refined and retains only a mild olive flavor.

Fruit Salad

Added sweetener or dressing isn't necessary when you mix colorful, flavorful fruit.

INGREDIENTS

½ cup honeydew cubes

½ cup cantaloupe cubes

½ cup seedless watermelon cubes

½ cup blueberries

½ cup pineapple cubes

½ cup strawberry slices

Combine all ingredients.

MAKES 3 CUPS

Calories: 64 | Fat: 0 g | Protein: 1 g | Fiber: 2 g

An Old-Fashioned Watermelon Basket

To make a fun presentation for fruit salad, cut a watermelon in half, and scoop out the pink flesh, leaving behind the green-and-white shell. Cut up the watermelon and other fruits, combine, and use the watermelon shell as your serving bowl.

Green Salad with Mock Caesar Dressing

Silken tofu can make a great addition to creamy dishes. Tofu takes the flavor of most foods that you place with it. In a dressing, your children will never know that they are eating tofu! Add Fresh Croutons from page 251.

INGREDIENTS

1 head of romaine lettuce, washed and torn

2 tomatoes, cut into wedges

2 garlic cloves

2 tablespoons Dijon mustard

12 ounces silken tofu

½ cup lemon juice

1 tablespoon Worcestershire sauce or vegan Worcestershire

1 teaspoon ground black pepper

1. Combine lettuce and tomatoes in large mixing bowl.

2. In a blender, combine remainder of ingredients and blend until smooth for dressing.

3. Toss salad with desired amount of dressing.

YIELDS 8 CUPS

Calories: 48 | Fat: 2 g | Protein: 3 g | Fiber: 2 g

Which Tofu to Pick?

There are different types of tofu: silken or soft, firm, and extra-firm. When following a tofu recipe, pay attention to the type of tofu it calls for. Silken tofu is best for puddings and dips, while stir-fry mostly uses firm tofu.

Lemony Rice and Asparagus Salad

Save extra dressing for leftover rice salad. Overnight, the rice will absorb the dressing and will benefit from the extra flavor.

INGREDIENTS

2 cups enriched white rice

4 cups water

1 bunch asparagus

2 tablespoons fresh dill

¼ cup olive oil

½ cup lemon juice

Asparagus, the Plant That Keeps on Giving

Asparagus is a perennial plant; it is a member of the lily family. Asparagus spears are the shoots that grow from a crown that is planted approximately 3 feet underground. Although the shoots or spears are not picked for the first three years, the same plant can produce spears for fifteen to twenty years.

1. In a medium saucepan, bring rice and water to a boil.

2. Reduce heat, cover, and simmer 20 minutes, or until liquid is absorbed.

3. Let rice sit covered 5 minutes before fluffing with a fork.

4. While rice cooks, clean asparagus and remove tough ends.

5. Chop asparagus into 1-inch pieces.

6. Steam asparagus until bright and tender.

7. Mince dill.

8. Combine olive oil and lemon juice in a lidded jar. Shake to combine.

9. Combine rice, asparagus, dill, and ½ cup of the dressing.

10. Chill before serving.

MAKES 4 CUPS (8 SERVINGS)

Calories: 241 | Fat: 7 g | Protein: 4 g | Fiber: 2 g

Mango Coleslaw

The collard greens and coleslaw can be cooked for this recipe if your child is not comfortable with the crunchy texture of the raw vegetables.

INGREDIENTS

3 stalks of collard greens

5 cups coleslaw prepared mix

3 ripe mangos or 3 cups frozen mango

¼ cup red onion, chopped

2 tablespoons olive oil

1 tablespoon gluten-free, casein-free balsamic vinegar

1 tablespoon light agave nectar

Why Are Collard Greens So Good for You?

Collard greens are excellent sources of vitamins K, A, and C. Furthermore, they are a good source of the nutrient manganese. What is manganese? It helps your body to be able to use the vitamin C that is in your diet. Manganese is also vital in the chemical processes that help create natural antioxidants in your body.

1. Chop collard greens into tiny pieces.

2. In large mixing bowl, combine coleslaw mixture, collard greens, mango, and onion.

3. In small mixing bowl, combine olive oil, vinegar, and agave nectar and mix well to create dressing.

4. Pour dressing over contents in large mixing bowl.

5. Toss and serve.

YIELDS 8 CUPS (6 SERVINGS)

Calories: 102 | Fat: 0 g | Protein: 2 g | Fiber: 4 g

Quinoa and Bean Salad

The key to successful quinoa is to thoroughly rinse your quinoa before you cook it. This rinsing helps the quinoa from becoming bitter tasting.

INGREDIENTS

1 cup rinsed quinoa

2 cups water

1 can of kidney beans

1 cup of frozen corn

1 red pepper, finely chopped

Juice of 1 lemon

⅓ cup cilantro, finely chopped

3 tablespoons gluten-free, casein-free balsamic vinegar

½ cup of olive oil

2 tablespoons of cumin

Salt to taste

1. Rinse the quinoa under cold running water until the water runs clear.

2. In a medium saucepan, place quinoa and water. Turn on medium heat and cook 10–15 minutes or until all the water is absorbed. Fluff with fork.

3. Combine quinoa with remaining ingredients. Mix thoroughly, chill, and serve.

YIELDS 6 CUPS (6 SERVINGS)

Calories: 443 | Fat: 22 g | Protein: 11 g | Fiber: 7 g

Quinoa Is a Complete Protein!

Protein is made up of tiny particles called amino acids. There are nine essential amino acids that our bodies need to obtain from food, since our bodies do not make them. Quinoa contains all nine of these essential amino acids! As long as your family eats a variety of food, you should be getting enough protein without worrying about combining foods to make complete proteins.

Roasted Potato Salad

Roasting potatoes adds some variety to the traditional boiled potatoes that are usually used in potato salads. Roasting is an easy process that adds a nice surprising flavor to your potato salad.

INGREDIENTS

2 pounds new potatoes

4 tablespoons gluten-free, casein-free Italian dressing

½ red onion, chopped

¼ cup gluten-free, casein-free Parmesan cheese (optional)

½ teaspoon sea salt

¼ teaspoon pepper

1. Cut raw potatoes into small bite-size pieces and toss with vinaigrette.

2. Arrange on a baking sheet and put into cold oven.

3. Heat up oven to 450°F and roast potatoes about 20–30 minutes. Turn potatoes over about halfway through the roasting process to allow even roasting.

4. Remove from oven and toss with remaining ingredients.

MAKES 4 CUPS

Calories: 89 | Fat: 7 g | Protein: 2 g | Fiber: 1 g

Tabbouleh Salad

The perfect summer salad. Make this salad at the peak of tomato season to use some of the best tomatoes produced all year!

INGREDIENTS

3 cups quinoa, cooked

1 cup cannellini beans

1½ cups parsley, finely chopped

3 large tomatoes

3 green onions, sliced

1 tablespoon mint, finely chopped

¼ cup extra-virgin olive oil

¼ cup lemon juice

1. Combine all ingredients.
2. Chill for 2–3 hours and then serve.

YIELDS 8 CUPS (6 SERVINGS)

Calories: 190 | Fat: 10 g | Protein: 6 g | Fiber: 4 g

Tofu Salad

Serve this cool, summery salad stuffed into a tomato or melon half. You can also serve it with gluten-free crackers or corn chips.

INGREDIENTS

1 pound firm or extra-firm tofu

½ cup gluten-free, casein-free mayonnaise

2 tablespoons prepared yellow mustard

½ teaspoon dried dill

¼ minced sweet onion, like Vidalia

½ cup shredded carrot

1. Mash tofu until crumbly with a fork.

2. Add remaining ingredients, stir to combine.

MAKES 3 CUPS (6 SERVINGS)

Calories: 220 | Fat: 20 g | Protein: 8 g | Fiber: 2 g

Tofu Storage

Store any leftover tofu in a sealed container. Fresh water should cover the tofu. Change the water every day, and the tofu should remain fresh for up to one week.

Traditional Potato Salad

*Combining sweet potatoes and russet potatoes
is a nice twist to a familiar dish.*

INGREDIENTS

4 russet potatoes

2 sweet potatoes

3 eggs

½ cup sweet green peas, cooked
from frozen or canned

2 scallion onions, chopped

½ cup gluten-free, casein-free
mayonnaise

1 tablespoon yellow mustard

Sea salt and pepper to taste

Are Sweet Potatoes Really Potatoes?

No! There are more than 100 varieties of edible potatoes but the sweet potato is not one of them! These two root vegetables are completely different! The potato's scientific name is *Solanum tuberosum*, and its relatives are tomatoes, eggplants, and peppers. The sweet potato's scientific name is *Ipomoea batatas*, and it is in another plant family. Sweet potatoes are more closely related to morning glories than they are to regular potatoes!

1. In a large saucepan, boil water for potatoes and boil until soft. Once soft, remove from heat and cut potatoes into bite-size pieces.

2. In small pot, cover eggs with cold water and bring to boil. Cover and remove from heat for approximately 10 minutes. Remove from water, cool, and chop.

3. Place eggs and potatoes in large mixing bowl.

4. Add remaining 5 ingredients and mix thoroughly.

5. Salt and pepper to taste at the end.

6. Refrigerate until served.

YIELDS 8 SERVINGS

Calories: 351 | Fat: 21 g | Protein: 15 g | Fiber: 3 g

Black Bean Slaw

And you thought coleslaw was just shredded cabbage! There are hundreds of different kinds of cabbage, and adding different ingredients and dressings gives you a wide variety of tasty options!

INGREDIENTS

2½ cups finely shredded cabbage

1 (15-ounce) can black beans, rinsed and drained

½ cup shredded carrot

½ cup chopped purple onion

¼ cup chopped fresh cilantro

½ cup gluten-free, casein-free plain soy yogurt

½ cup salsa

2 tablespoons gluten-free, casein-free mayonnaise

2 teaspoons white wine vinegar

2 teaspoons lime juice

Fresh cilantro sprigs (optional)

1. In a large bowl, combine cabbage, beans, carrot, onion, and chopped cilantro. Toss well.

2. In a small bowl, combine soy yogurt, salsa, mayonnaise, vinegar, and lime juice. Stir well. Pour over cabbage mixture and gently toss.

3. Tightly cover. Refrigerate at least 2 hours. Garnish with fresh cilantro sprigs if desired.

SERVES 8

Calories: 109 | Fat: 3 g | Protein: 5 g | Fiber: 5 g

Veggie Slaw

A dish with fresh red cabbage always makes a pretty addition to a table setting, and it's a double win when it tastes great too!

INGREDIENTS

1½ cups shredded red cabbage

1 cup shredded carrot

¾ cup shredded yellow squash

¾ cup shredded zucchini

½ cup chopped green pepper

⅓ cup finely chopped onion

¼ cup unsweetened pineapple juice

1½ tablespoons sugar

3 tablespoons cider vinegar

2 tablespoons water

½ teaspoon gluten-free, casein-free chicken-flavored bouillon granules

¼ teaspoon paprika

¼ teaspoon celery seeds

⅛ teaspoon garlic powder

Dash of ground red pepper

1. In a large bowl, combine cabbage, carrot, yellow squash, zucchini, green pepper, and chopped onion.

2. In a small bowl, combine pineapple juice, sugar, vinegar, water, bouillon, paprika, celery seeds, garlic powder, and red pepper. Stir well.

3. Pour over vegetable mixture. Toss gently.

4. Cover tightly and refrigerate at least 4 hours before serving. Toss gently at serving time.

SERVES 4

Calories: 63 | Fat: 0 g | Protein: 2 g | Fiber: 3 g

Red Cabbage Trivia

Some people call red cabbage by a slightly different name—purple cabbage. Its color does change according to the environment it's in; it will even turn blue if served with nonacidic food. All colors aside, red cabbage happens to be much higher in vitamin C than other types of cabbage.

Wild Rice Cranberry Salad

The vividness of this salad is second only to its incredible tastiness! Serve chilled or at room temperature.

INGREDIENTS

6 ounces wild rice, uncooked

6 ounces fresh cranberries

¼ cup cranberry juice cocktail

1 tablespoon sugar

½ cup carrots cut in strips

1 cup minced green onions

1 tablespoon apple cider vinegar

2 teaspoons peanut oil

Dash freshly ground pepper

1. Prepare rice according to package directions. Set aside.

2. Combine cranberries, juice, and sugar in a medium saucepan. Cook over medium heat. Stir occasionally until cranberries pop, about 5 minutes.

3. Remove from heat and cool slightly.

4. Transfer cranberry mixture to a large mixing bowl. Add remaining ingredients. Toss gently until combined well.

5. Cover and refrigerate until serving time.

SERVES 4

Calories: 222 | Fat: 3 g | Protein: 7 g | Fiber: 6 g

CHAPTER 8

Enticing Entrees

Baja-Style Fish Tacos

*The spice in this dish can be increased by increasing the
amount of jalapeño peppers or the cayenne pepper.
This sauce is on the low end of the spice range for children.*

INGREDIENTS

1 teaspoon canola oil

1 pound cod; cut into 2-ounce
portions

1 lime, juiced

¾ teaspoon sea salt; divided

½ cup gluten-free, casein-free
sour cream

½ cup gluten-free, casein-free
mayonnaise

2 limes, juiced

½ fresh jalapeño pepper,
deseeded, halved, and
deribbed

½ teaspoon dried oregano

½ teaspoon dried dill weed

¼ teaspoon ground cumin

¼ teaspoon cayenne

8 gluten-free corn tortillas

½ medium head cabbage, finely
shredded

½ medium head red cabbage,
finely shredded

1. Lightly oil a shallow baking dish
   with 1 teaspoon canola oil. Arrange
   fish in dish.

2. Sprinkle fish with the juice of 1 lime
   and ½ teaspoon sea salt. Cover
   with foil and bake at 400°F for 10–
   15 minutes. Remove from oven
   when done.

3. In a blender, combine ¼ teaspoon
   sea salt and next 8 ingredients to
   form sauce for tacos.

4. Heat corn tortillas lightly in skillet
   on stove, top with portion of
   cooked fish, drizzle with sauce, and
   place handful of both types of
   finely shredded cabbage on top.
   Serve.

MAKES 8 TACOS

Calories: 258 | Fat: 15 g | Protein: 13 g | Fiber: 4 g

How Hot Is Your Pepper?

The hotness of peppers is measured by the
Scoville scale, which was developed by Wilbur
Scoville in 1912. The range goes from 0 Scoville
units to 16,000,000 Scoville units. The bell pepper is a 0 and the habanero is a 200,000. The
jalapeño in this recipe scores about 5,000.

BBQ Fish

There are many fish whose depletion is endangering the environment. Some of the most common and environmentally friendly fish are Alaskan wild salmon, white sea bass, U.S.-farmed tilapia, and U.S.-farmed catfish.

INGREDIENTS

4 fillets of Alaska longline cod

1 cup gluten-free, casein-free barbecue sauce

12 slices onion

1. Preheat oven to 350°F.

2. Lay out 4 pieces of foil or parchment paper, each large enough to wrap around one fillet.

3. On each piece of foil or parchment paper, spread out ¼ cup barbecue sauce and 3 slices of onion, then lay a fillet in the center.

4. Fold up foil or paper and bake for about 10–15 minutes.

MAKES 4 FILLETS

Calories: 360 | Fat: 2 g | Protein: 41 g | Fiber: 0 g

Barbecue Meatloaf Muffins

The flaxseed meal is acting as an egg replacer in this recipe.

INGREDIENTS

1 tablespoon flaxseed meal

3 tablespoons water

1½ pounds 95 percent lean organic ground beef

1 cup tomato juice

¾ cup rolled gluten-free oats

¼ cup chopped onion

2 garlic cloves, minced

2 tablespoons oregano

1½ cups gluten-free, casein-free barbecue sauce

Flaxseed Meal Can Replace Eggs!

Flaxseed meal can be used to replace the egg that is traditionally used in meatloaf! Flax meal is a source of omega-3 essential fatty acids, which are often low in the American diet. There is good evidence to show that flaxseed is good for improving overall general health and preventing diseases.

1. Mix flaxseed meal and water. Stir and allow to sit for 2–3 minutes.

2. Preheat oven to 350°F.

3. Combine meat, tomato juice, rolled oats, onion, garlic, and oregano. Add flaxseed meal and water combination to this mixture and knead until well mixed.

4. Portion out into a regular-size muffin tin. Top each muffin with 2 tablespoons barbecue sauce.

5. Bake until internal temperature of 160°F is reached.

MAKES 12 MUFFINS

Calories: 149 | Fat: 4 g | Protein: 13 g | Fiber: 1 g

Beef Brochettes

If you are using bamboo skewers, soak them in water for about 1 hour before using to help prevent burning or catching them on fire while grilling.

INGREDIENTS

1 cup steak sauce

¼ cup Italian dressing

¼ cup agave nectar

1 garlic clove, minced

1 pound beef sirloin or sirloin steak

1 red bell pepper, cut into squares

1 green bell pepper, cut into squares

1 pineapple, cut into squares

1. In blender, combine first 4 ingredients. Blend until smooth. Pour into glass baking dish.
2. Cut beef into cubes and place beef in the baking dish, cover, and marinade overnight.
3. Alternate meat, pepper, pineapple, pepper on a skewer.
4. Grill until done. Remove from skewer before giving to children.

MAKES 7 SKEWERS

Calories: 200 | Fat: 4 g | Protein: 9 g | Fiber: 3 g

Skewer Tips

You can also soak the skewers in beef broth for 1 hour, which will provide more flavor while cooking. Or coat the skewer lightly with canola oil, which can withstand the high heat of the grill. Instead of putting meat and vegetables on same skewer, separate onto 2 different skewers since they have different cooking times.

Broccolini with Meat and Rigatoni

The meat in this dish can easily be omitted for a vegetarian dish.

INGREDIENTS

1 pound gluten-free, casein-free brown rice rigatoni pasta

½ pound ground beef

4 tablespoons olive oil

1 tablespoon gluten-free, casein-free margarine

4 garlic cloves, minced

1 bunch broccolini separated into florets

1 cup gluten-free, casein-free broth (vegetable, chicken, or beef)

1 cup fresh basil, coarsely chopped, divided

Fresh parsley, chopped

Vegan Parmesan cheese (optional)

1. Cook rigatoni pasta according to directions, drain, and set aside.

2. In medium pan, cook ground beef in small amount of olive oil. Drain and set aside.

3. In a large skillet, heat oil and margarine. Sauté garlic until browned over medium heat. Add broccolini and stir gently until the pan gets very hot.

4. Add chicken broth and simmer until broccolini is al dente.

5. Add half the basil, drained rigatoni, and ground beef to skillet and mix thoroughly.

6. Transfer to serving bowl, top with remaining basil, parsley, and Parmesan cheese.

YIELDS 8 CUPS

Calories: 347 | Fat: 11 g | Protein: 14 g | Fiber: 2 g

Chicken and Broccoli Stir-Fry

If broccoli is in season, use fresh organic vegetables.
Combine broccoli, water chestnuts, baby corn, and red peppers
and make your own stir-fry mixture!

INGREDIENTS

1 pound boneless, skinless chicken breasts

2 garlic cloves, minced

3 tablespoons honey

1 tablespoon light agave nectar

2 tablespoons low-sodium soy sauce

2 tablespoons orange juice

½ teaspoon fresh ginger, grated

⅛ teaspoon sea salt

⅛ teaspoon black pepper

1 package frozen broccoli stir-fry mix (broccoli, water chestnuts, peppers, corn)

2 teaspoons cornstarch

4 cups brown rice, cooked

The Origin of Stir-Frying!

Stir-frying developed during a period of time in China where cooking materials and food were in short supply. Items had to be cooked fast without wasting any food and with minimum fuel. Now, we know it is a healthful way to cook vegetables and preserve their nutrients.

1. Cut chicken into small strips. Combine next 8 ingredients in a medium bowl and marinate the chicken for 1 hour.

2. In a large, lightly oiled skillet, stir-fry chicken and marinade until chicken turns light brown and is done. Remove from skillet but keep warm.

3. In same skillet, stir-fry the vegetables until heated through and return chicken and marinade to pan. In small bowl, combine cornstarch and cold water and mix until there are no lumps.

4. Place cornstarch in pan with chicken and vegetables. Allow this to come to a boil and cook for 1–2 minutes or until thickened.

5. Serve over brown rice.

MAKES 8 CUPS

Calories: 238 | Fat: 2 g | Protein: 17 g | Fiber: 3 g

Chicken and Rice Noodles

The spices in this dish can vary! Add more red pepper flakes for adult dishes and keep the spice minimal if your children are not used to spicy food.

INGREDIENTS

1 pound boneless, skinless chicken breasts

2 cans crushed pineapple in natural juices

9-ounce package of long rice noodles, such as fettuccine

¾ cup sunflower-seed butter

½ cup light coconut milk

½ cup gluten-free, casein-free vegetable or chicken broth

2½ ounces carrot puree or carrot baby food

2 teaspoons garlic, minced

½ teaspoon ground ginger

2 tablespoons fresh lime juice

⅛ teaspoon red pepper flakes (optional)

1. Preheat oven to 350°F. Arrange chicken in 9" × 13" baking dish and pour in pineapple juice from crushed pineapple. Cover and bake until internal temperature reaches 170°F.

2. In large pot, boil about 8 cups of water. Once boiling, place rice noodles in water and boil until tender, approximately 8–10 minutes. Drain noodles and rinse with cold water.

3. While pasta is cooking, blend remaining 8 ingredients in blender until smooth. Use extra broth to thin to desired consistency.

4. Return noodles to cooking pot and pour contents of blender into noodles and stir.

5. Cut or shred chicken into age-appropriate-size pieces for your children; top with crushed pineapple. Serve with a side of the rice noodles with sunflower-seed butter sauce.

MAKES 10 SERVINGS

Calories: 308 | Fat: 14 g | Protein: 15 g | Fiber: 1 g

Easy Baked Chicken

In this simple but delicious recipe, the yogurt protects the chicken from becoming dry and gives it a nice flavor. Mix the yogurt with your favorite seasoning, or a gluten-free, casein-free barbecue sauce for a fun twist.

INGREDIENTS

1 pound boneless, skinless chicken breasts

1 (12-ounce) container of gluten-free, casein-free plain soy yogurt

1. Preheat oven to 350°F.

2. Coat chicken with yogurt and place in baking dish.

3. Bake covered in aluminum foil for 10 minutes.

4. Remove foil and allow chicken to complete cooking uncovered. About 10 more minutes.

YIELDS 4 CHICKEN BREASTS

Calories: 203 | Fat: 3 g | Protein: 29 g | Fiber: 1 g

Baked Honey Pescado

*This makes a very sweet fish. Children gobble it up, but adults may like it with the following modifications:
no agave nectar and 2½ tablespoons of Dijon mustard.*

INGREDIENTS

2 tablespoons wildflower honey

1 tablespoon light agave nectar

1½ tablespoons gluten-free, casein-free mustard

1½ tablespoons gluten-free, casein-free mayonnaise

1 teaspoon lemon juice

Sprinkle of sea salt

1 pound white sea bass

1. Preheat oven to 400°F.

2. In small bowl, combine first 6 ingredients.

3. Place fish in a lightly oiled shallow baking dish

4. Spread mixture on top of fish.

5. Bake for 15 minutes or until fish flakes lightly with a fork.

MAKES 4 SERVINGS

Calories: 198 | Fat: 7 g | Protein: 21 g | Fiber: 0 g

Looking for White Sea Bass in Your Local Store?

It often goes by a few different names such as king croaker, weakfish, or sea trout. This fish is typically caught in the wild off the Pacific Coast of the United States. It is a firm whitish fish that has a mild flavor. This is a good choice for seafood, as it is not overfished and is not at risk for high mercury contamination.

Horseradish Brisket

This is an excellent recipe for parties, holidays, or large gatherings. It is a large, crowd-pleasing dish! Serve this with Mashed Potatoes on page 195 and the Green Salad with Mock Cesar Dressing on page 106.

INGREDIENTS

3–5 pounds beef brisket

1 jar (6-ounces) horseradish spread or 3 ounces fresh horseradish

1 jar (12-ounces) gluten-free, casein-free barbecue sauce

1. Preheat oven to 250°F.

2. Roll out foil to a size large enough to wrap around the whole brisket.

3. Place beef brisket in center of foil and cover with horseradish and gluten-free, casein-free barbecue sauce.

4. Fold up foil and bake for about 5–6 hours, until done.

SERVES 8–10

Calories: 448 | Fat: 15 g | Protein: 59 g | Fiber: 1 g

Farmer's Pie

This casserole is well suited for young diners, as it has a very tender consistency and a hint of sweetness thanks to the sweet potatoes.

INGREDIENTS

2 large sweet potatoes

1 tablespoon olive oil

¼ cup grated onion

¼ cup grated zucchini

¼ cup grated carrot

2 cloves garlic, minced

1 pound 95 percent lean ground turkey or beef or gluten- and casein-free veggie burger crumbles

½ cup gluten-free, casein-free plain soy yogurt

½ teaspoon salt

Gluten-free Veggie Burger Crumbles

Be careful! Many veggie burgers are made from a combination of wheat gluten and soy protein. Look for a statement on the box ensuring that the veggie burgers you are choosing are gluten- and casein-free. To make crumbles, chop up thawed veggie burgers and then cook according to your recipe's directions.

1. Preheat oven to 350°F.

2. Peel and dice sweet potatoes.

3. In a large saucepan, cover sweet potatoes with water.

4. Bring to a boil; boil uncovered until tender, approximately 10 minutes.

5. While potatoes are cooking, heat olive oil in a medium skillet.

6. Add garlic and vegetables. Sauté until soft, 5 minutes.

7. Add veggie burger crumbles and heat through.

8. When sweet potatoes are tender, drain and return them to the pot.

9. Mash the sweet potatoes with yogurt and salt using a potato masher or fork.

10. Scrape the burger mixture into a 3-quart casserole.

11. Spread the sweet potatoes on top.

12. Bake uncovered for 40 minutes.

MAKES A 3-QUART CASSEROLE (SERVES 6)

Calories: 217 | Fat: 10 g | Protein: 17 g | Fiber: 2 g

Pork and Beans

Serve this on your favorite gluten-free rolls and top with a small amount of barbecue sauce. Try this also as a side dish. Serve this pork and beans with fresh fruit salad or the Mango Coleslaw found on page 108.

INGREDIENTS

2 pounds boneless pork ribs

14 ounces gluten-free, casein-free beef broth

1 (12-ounce) bottle gluten-free, casein-free mild barbecue sauce, divided

1 can black beans, drained

Rethink the Recipe

Pork and beans does not have to be chopped hot dogs and pinto beans! Adding spices and vegetables such as roasted red peppers, tomatoes, green peppers, and onions can also give your pulled pork a little kick. This pulled pork and bean mixture can also be wrapped in corn tortillas and topped with shredded cabbage to make a nice pork taco.

1. In slow cooker, place pork ribs and beef broth. Cook on high for about 4 hours.

2. Once done, remove pork from cooker and shred pork.

3. In small saucepan, heat black beans until heated through.

4. Mix pork with 6 ounces barbecue sauce and black beans.

MAKES 6 CUPS (SERVES 6–8)

Calories: 402 | Fat: 17 g | Protein: 34 g | Fiber: 3 g

Chicken Corn Bites

These corn-coated chicken bites are a nice addition to your child's menus!
Bring a taste of the south to your table.

INGREDIENTS

½ cup canola oil

2 cups cornmeal

¼ teaspoon hot paprika

½ teaspoon garlic salt

1 pound boneless, skinless chicken
  breasts, cut into strips

2 eggs, beaten

1. Heat canola oil in a medium skillet over high heat.

2. Blend cornmeal in your blender until it is a fine flour, add paprika and garlic salt, and blend well.

3. Dip chicken strips in eggs, put in bag with cornmeal, and shake.

4. Fry chicken strips in oil until done; drain on paper towels and serve.

MAKES 16 BITES

Calories: 144 | Fat: 5 g | Protein: 9 g | Fiber: 1 g

Shepherd's Pie

Be sure to check the labels on your Dijon mustard and Worcestershire sauce to ensure that they are gluten- and casein-free.

INGREDIENTS

3 large potatoes, peeled

1 tablespoon olive oil

1 red onion, chopped

½ cup diced carrots

1½ pounds ground beef

2 tablespoons flaxseed meal

¾ cup gluten-free, casein-free beef broth

¾ cup green peas

¾ cup corn

1 teaspoon Worcestershire sauce

1 teaspoon ketchup

1 teaspoon Dijon mustard

2 tablespoons gluten-free, casein-free margarine

½ cup gluten-free, casein-free soy milk

1. In a large pot bring to a boil enough water to cover potatoes. Cut potatoes and place in boiling water.

2. In large skillet, heat 1 tablespoon olive oil. Sauté onions and carrots until tender. Add ground beef and flaxseed meal to pan and brown. Drain beef and return to hot skillet.

3. Add next 6 ingredients to skillet and heat for about 10 minutes.

4. Meanwhile, remove potatoes from boiling water when tender. Mash with margarine and soy milk. Be careful not to make these potatoes too thin.

5. In a 9" × 13" pan, first layer and press meat mixture into the bottom of pan evenly. Then for the top layer, spread mashed potatoes on the top of meat mixture. Use a fork to arrange the potatoes into an even but pointy layer. There should be peaks of potatoes sticking up to get brown.

6. Bake at 400°F for 30 minutes. Broil for 5 minutes at the end to crisp.

MAKES 10 SERVINGS

Calories: 275 | Fat: 11 g | Protein: 18 g | Fiber: 4 g

Taco Dinner

This recipe has very little spice to it for those children who don't like spicy food. To make it spicier, pull your child's portion out of the skillet, then add your hot sauce, peppers, and green chilies to the remaining meat.

INGREDIENTS

1 pound 95 percent lean ground beef or turkey

1 cup frozen corn, thawed

12 corn taco shells

2 cups shredded green cabbage

2 whole avocados, sliced

1 cup diced tomatoes

Forget Taco Seasoning Packets!

Make your own taco seasoning mixture! Mix the following: 1 tablespoon chili powder; ¼ teaspoon each of garlic powder, onion powder, crushed red pepper flakes, and dried oregano; ½ teaspoon each of cumin and paprika; and 1 teaspoon each of sea salt and black pepper.

1. In a medium skillet, brown ground beef and drain.

2. Return to skillet and add corn to ground beef and heat.

3. Heat corn taco shells in the oven to crisp up.

4. Top each taco with beef and corn mixture, shredded cabbage, avocado slices, and tomatoes. Serve.

MAKES 12 TACOS

Calories: 171 | Fat: 10 g | Protein: 3 g | Fiber: 4 g

Rotini with Bolognese Sauce

In Italy, bowls of pasta are layered differently! The sauce is the most important part of the meal, so the pasta is added to the sauce, instead of the sauce being added on top of the pasta!

INGREDIENTS

2 tablespoons olive oil

2 tablespoons gluten-free, casein-free margarine

½ Vidalia onion, diced

½ celery stalk, diced

½ carrot diced

1 pound ground beef

15 ounces gluten-free, casein-free tomato sauce

2 tablespoons gluten-free tomato paste

4 cups gluten-free rotini, cooked

Gluten-free, casein-free Parmesan cheese, optional

1. In a large pot, over medium heat, heat olive oil and margarine.

2. Add onion, celery, and carrots and sauté until onion is clear.

3. Add ground beef and cook thoroughly.

4. Add tomato sauce and paste and heat through.

5. Mix rotini and sauce, top with Parmesan cheese if using, and serve.

MAKES 2 CUPS OF SAUCE (SERVES 8)

Calories: 285 | Fat: 12 g | Protein: 16 g | Fiber: 4 g

Want to Have Lunch in Rome?

In Italy, lunch is the largest meal of the day, often with many courses. Breakfast is typically very small amounts, and dinner tends to be much smaller portions of leftovers from lunch. Italian diets are rich in whole grains, vegetables, fish, and olive oil. This pattern of eating is often associated with low rates of heart disease.

Savory Rice and Sausage

This is so easy and really great for any time when you are really busy.
Kids love it and grownups do too.
To lighten the fat content, use a turkey sausage.

INGREDIENTS

1 pound gluten-free, casein-free Italian sausage, sweet or hot, cut into 1-inch pieces

1 medium onion, chopped fine

2 cloves garlic, chopped

1 cup white rice

2¾ cups gluten-free, casein-free chicken broth

1 teaspoon dried rosemary, or 1 tablespoon fresh rosemary

Gluten-free, casein-free Parmesan cheese (optional) and chopped fresh parsley to garnish

1. Brown the sausage pieces, onion, and garlic. If the sausage is very lean, add a bit of olive oil to prevent the food from sticking.

2. Stir in the rice and toss with the sausage and vegetables. Add the broth and rosemary and cover. In a broiler-safe skillet or casserole dish, cook on very low heat or place in a 325°F oven for 45 minutes to 1 hour, depending on the type of rice you are using. (Do not use instant rice.)

3. Just before serving, sprinkle the top with Parmesan cheese and brown under the broiler. Add the chopped parsley and serve.

SERVES 4–6

Calories: 482 | Fat: 29 g | Protein: 19 g | Fiber: 1 g

Crispy Potato-Crusted Chicken

When you use this crust on your baked chicken, you'll find it's really crispy and crunchy. Don't add salt as potato chips are already salty.

INGREDIENTS

4 ounces potato chips

4 boneless, skinless chicken breasts

⅔ cup gluten-free, casein-free sour cream

1 teaspoon freshly ground black pepper

2 tablespoons snipped fresh chives

1 teaspoon dried thyme

Alternatives to Bread-crumbs

Try using your food processor to make crumbs of such goodies as cornbread, potato chips, or popcorn. Check various rice cereals such as puffed rice and rice crisps to make sure they are gluten-free, then put them in your food processor to make crumbs. Store the crumbs in resealable plastic bags in the refrigerator.

1. In a food processor, chop up potato chips until you have 1 cup of crumbs.

2. Rinse the chicken, dry on paper towels, and lay it in a baking dish that you have prepared with nonstick spray.

3. Preheat the oven to 350°F. Spread the chicken with sour cream, sprinkle with the potato chip crumbs mixed with the pepper, chives, and thyme, and bake for 25 minutes or until brown and crispy.

SERVES 4

Calories: 457 | Fat: 29 g | Protein: 33 g | Fiber: 1 g

The Best Roasted Turkey

For the sweetest, juiciest bird, try to find a turkey that is between 9 and 12 pounds. Make extra gravy by adding a can of chicken broth to the basting liquid.

INGREDIENTS

1 10-pound turkey

¼ cup olive oil

1 teaspoon dried thyme

½ cup fresh Italian flat-leaf parsley, rinsed and minced

Salt to taste and 1 teaspoon pepper

Giblets, including wing tips and neck

½ cup gluten-free, casein-free chicken broth

2 bay leaves

1 recipe Stuffing for Roasted Turkey (page 204)

4 strips bacon for bottom of roasting pan

2 teaspoons cornstarch

¼ cup water

1. Rinse the turkey in cold water and pat dry. Mix the olive oil, herbs, salt, and pepper thoroughly. Tease it under the skin of the breast, being careful not to tear the skin.

2. Place the giblets and wing tips in a saucepan with the broth and water to cover. Add the bay leaves. Cook for 2 hours, or while the turkey is cooking. Add extra water if the broth gets dry.

3. Stuff the turkey and skewer the legs together. Close the neck cavity with a skewer. Preheat the oven to 325°F.

4. Put the bacon on the bottom of the roasting pan and start the turkey breast-side down. After 30 minutes, turn the turkey over. Arrange bacon over the breast and legs. Roast for 3 hours, basting every 20 minutes with the giblet stock and juices. Roast until the thickest part is 165°F.

5. Make gravy by mixing 2 teaspoons cornstarch with ¼ cup water and blending with pan juices.

SERVES 15

For Turkey only:
Calories: 241 | Fat: 10 g | Protein: 34 g | Fiber: 0 g

Roasting Turkeys

Always start the turkey breast-side down so the juices run into, rather than out of, the breast. The bacon prevents the breast from sticking to the roasting pan and adds a nice flavor to the juices. If, like most families, you like extra dressing (stuffing), make 3 to 4 cups extra and roast it in a casserole while you are roasting the turkey.

Sesame-Crusted Chicken Breasts

Serve this with rice and lots of vegetables.
Leftovers can be chopped, mixed with a spicy sauce,
and used to fill Basic Crepes (page 48) as a delicious snack.

INGREDIENTS

¼ cup pineapple juice

¼ cup orange juice

1 tablespoon lime juice

½ cup gluten-free, casein-free soy sauce

1 inch gingerroot, peeled and minced

2 cloves garlic, or to taste, minced

1 teaspoon chili oil, or to taste (optional)

2 large boneless, skinless chicken breasts, halved

1 egg, beaten

½ cup sesame seeds

1. In a nonreactive bowl or glass pan large enough to hold the chicken, whisk together the juices, soy sauce, ginger, garlic, and chili oil. Rinse the chicken breasts and pat dry with paper towels. Add the chicken to the sauce and turn to coat. Cover and refrigerate for 4 hours.

2. Drain the chicken; dip in beaten egg and then in sesame seeds. Grill or sauté in oil for 6 minutes per side, depending on thickness of meat. Serve hot.

SERVES 4

Calories: 440 | Fat: 27 g | Protein: 24 g | Fiber: 4 g

Chili and Other Hot Sauces

The Chinese, Indians, and other groups in Asia, Southeast Asia, and Asia Minor make their own versions of chili for cooking. Chili oil is extremely hot. Chili paste comes in green and red and is popular in Thailand. The Chinese make a chili-and-garlic paste that is called Sichuan chili. Tabasco sauce, fresh chopped chilies (red and/or green), cayenne pepper, and red pepper flakes can be substituted. If your family does not like spice, it works well to leave out the chilies too!

Chicken Nuggets

These are a great snack for a group of children. Your guests will not know they are being served special gluten- and casein-free chicken nuggets!

INGREDIENTS

½ cup canola oil

3 cups Rice Chex cereal (crushed)

¼ teaspoon hot paprika

½ teaspoon garlic salt

1 pound boneless, skinless chicken breasts, cut into strips

2 eggs, beaten

1. Heat canola oil in a medium skillet over high heat.

2. Place Rice Chex in gallon-size plastic bag and crush; add paprika and garlic salt to bag and blend well.

3. Dip chicken strips in eggs, put in bag with Rice Chex and shake.

4. Fry chicken strips in oil until done, drain on paper towels and serve.

YIELDS 16 NUGGETS

Calories: 92 | Fat: 5 g | Protein: 8 g | Fiber: 0 g

Fish Baked in Papillote

Fish is an excellent source of omega-3 fatty acids, which are great for overall health and important for healthy brains! Go to www.sheddaquarium .org/pdf/Shedd_08_Right_Bite_card.pdf for lists of safe and unsafe fish.

INGREDIENTS

4 teaspoons olive oil

8 sprigs fresh rosemary

4 fillets of Pacific Halibut

4 teaspoons capers

2 large tomatoes

1. Preheat oven to 350°F.

2. Lay out 4 pieces of parchment paper, each large enough to wrap around one fillet.

3. On each piece of parchment paper, spread out 1 teaspoon olive oil and 2 sprigs of rosemary.

4. Add 1 fillet on top of rosemary, top with capers and tomatoes.

5. Fold up paper and bake for about 10–15 minutes.

YIELDS 4 FILLETS

Calories: 276 | Fat: 9 g | Protein: 43 g | Fiber: 1 g

CHAPTER 9

Vegetarian Entrees

Arroz Verde con Frijoles Negro

For a fun twist, serve this dish
with warmed corn tortillas instead of forks.

INGREDIENTS

5 cups gluten-free, casein-free vegetable broth, divided

1 bay leaf

2 cups short-grain brown rice

1 bunch spinach

2 tablespoons lemon juice

2 garlic cloves

2 cups cooked black beans

Pepper to taste

International Year of Rice

2004 was the International Year of Rice. This special year was marked with events in Asia, Europe, Latin America, Africa, and North America.

1. In a large saucepan, bring 4½ cups vegetable broth, bay leaf, and rice to a boil.

2. Reduce heat, cover, and simmer 40 minutes.

3. While rice is cooking, thoroughly wash spinach and remove stems.

4. Combine spinach, lemon juice, and garlic in food processor.

5. Process into a paste adding vegetable broth when necessary.

6. Remove bay leaf from rice, fluff with a fork, stir in drained and rinsed beans and spinach mixture.

7. Add pepper to taste.

MAKES 6 CUPS (6 SERVINGS)

Calories: 327 | Fat: 2 g | Protein: 11 g | Fiber: 9 g

Barbecue Tofu and Quinoa

*Quinoa and tofu combine for a
protein-rich meal with a lot of flavor.*

INGREDIENTS

1 cup quinoa

1 pound firm or extra-firm tofu

1 cup mushroom caps (button or
cremini)

¼ small onion

1 large red bell pepper

1 tablespoon olive oil

½ cup gluten-free, casein-free
barbecue sauce

Simple Barbecue Sauce

To make a tasty, basic barbecue sauce, combine ¼ cup soy
sauce, 2 tablespoons blackstrap molasses, 3 tablespoons
honey or agave nectar, and ¼
cup ketchup.

1. Thoroughly rinse 1 cup quinoa.

2. In a small saucepan, combine
   quinoa and 2 cups water. Bring to a
   boil.

3. Reduce heat to simmer, cover, and
   cook 15 minutes.

4. Cut tofu into 1-inch cubes.

5. Dice mushrooms, onion, and red
   pepper.

6. Heat olive oil over high heat, then
   add tofu. Cook 3 minutes, turning
   tofu as it cooks.

7. Add vegetables and cook 5 minutes
   more.

8. Add sauce and cook 5 more
   minutes.

9. Serve tofu over quinoa.

MAKES 5 CUPS OF BARBECUE TOFU

Calories: 247 | Fat: 13 g | Protein: 11 g | Fiber: 4 g

Black Bean Cakes

You can substitute cornmeal for gluten-free breadcrumbs in this recipe.

INGREDIENTS

2 cups cooked black beans (or 1 [15-ounce] can)

3 tablespoons mild salsa

2 tablespoons cornmeal or gluten-free, casein-free breadcrumbs

1 tablespoon canola oil

Change Things Up!

Changing side dishes can completely change the tone of a meal. If you serve black bean cakes with a side of rice and avocado one day, try serving them for breakfast with fried or scrambled eggs the next time. Once you find something that your child likes, you can expand on that by serving the favored dish with different foods.

1. Drain and rinse black beans.

2. Mash beans with a potato masher or fork.

3. Combine with salsa and breadcrumbs.

4. Form into small cakes.

5. In a medium skillet, heat oil over medium-high heat.

6. Cook cakes on each side.

MAKES 6 CAKES

Calories: 113 | Fat: 3 g | Protein: 5 g | Fiber: 6 g

Broccoli Quinoa Casserole

This dish is a comfort food that is great for a younger child but will please the rest of the family. Imagine Food's Organic Sweet Corn Soup has a nice consistency for this recipe. Or use the Creamy Corn Chowder on page 66.

INGREDIENTS

1 cup vegan creamy corn soup

½ cup gluten-free, casein-free soy Cheddar cheese

1 large bunch of broccoli

3 cups cooked quinoa

Is Quinoa a Grain?

Although quinoa looks like a grain and cooks like a grain, it is not a true cereal grain. It is actually the seeds of the Chenopodium, or goosefoot plant. Its relatives include beets, spinach, and Swiss chard.

1. In a small saucepan, heat soup over medium-high heat.

2. Add cheese and stir until melted. Set aside.

3. Cut broccoli into small florets and steam until tender.

4. Combine quinoa, cheese sauce, and broccoli.

MAKES 6 CUPS

Calories: 218 | Fat: 4 g | Protein: 8 g | Fiber: 6 g

Caribbean Baked Risotto

This dish is a complete meal incorporating fruit, vegetable, protein, and grain.

INGREDIENTS

1 cup Arborio rice

½ cup cooked black beans

1 garlic clove

1 cup coconut milk

3 cups gluten-free, casein-free broth (vegetable, chicken, or beef)

½ cup cooked pumpkin

1 cup pineapple pieces

1 cup chopped spinach

1. Preheat oven to 325°F.

2. Rinse rice.

3. Drain and rinse beans.

4. Mince garlic.

5. Combine all ingredients in a covered casserole.

6. Bake 1 hour.

MAKES 4½ CUPS (6 SERVINGS)

Calories: 270 | Fat: 9 g | Protein: 6 g | Fiber: 4 g

Risotto

Risotto is a traditional Italian creamy rice dish. It is typically made by stirring a small amount of hot liquid, usually broth or stock, into Arborio rice until the liquid is absorbed. This process continues until all of the liquid has been absorbed and the rice is fully cooked with a creamy, starch sauce. Baking Arborio rice brings about a similar result without standing in front of a stove for close to an hour. (A luxury not many parents can afford!)

Cheesy Polenta with Roasted Vegetables

*Combining the creamy polenta with the
tender roasted vegetables yields a comforting stew.*

INGREDIENTS

2 carrots

4 asparagus spears

6 mushrooms (button or cremini)

2 tablespoons olive oil

⅛ teaspoon salt

1 cup polenta or grits

3 cups water

½ cup gluten-free, casein-free soy
Cheddar cheese

Polenta, the Pasta of Northern Italy

Although Italy is known as the home of pasta and pizza, corn polenta has been a basic food-stuff since the late fifteenth century. Because corn, intro-duced to Italy from the New World, grows most easily in Northern Italy, polenta quickly became a culinary mainstay. It continues to be a very impor-tant component of Northern Italian cooking.

1. Preheat oven to 425°F.

2. Peel carrots and cut into ¼-inch-wide matchsticks.

3. Break off tough ends of asparagus, and cut into 1-inch-long pieces.

4. Cut mushrooms in half.

5. Toss vegetables in olive oil and salt. Spread on baking sheet and cook until tender, approximately 10–15 minutes.

6. While vegetables are cooking, bring water to a boil in a medium saucepan.

7. Slowly whisk in polenta and keep whisking until polenta thickens and pulls away from the sides of the pan.

8. Sprinkle on cheese, and stir to melt.

9. In a large bowl, stir to combine polenta and vegetables.

MAKES 5 CUPS (SERVES 4)

Calories: 240 | Fat: 9 g | Protein: 5 g | Fiber: 3 g

Corn Cakes with Black Bean Salsa

Serve each of these cornmeal pancakes with a dollop of the black bean salsa for a fun, breakfast-style dinner.

INGREDIENTS

¼ cup cornmeal

½ cup gluten-free all-purpose flour

½ teaspoon xanthan gum

1 tablespoon flaxseed meal

2 tablespoons water

½ cup creamy corn soup

¼ cup gluten-free, casein-free soy milk

2 teaspoons gluten-free, casein-free margarine

1 cup mild salsa

¼ cup cooked black beans

Save Those Jars!

Jarred salsa tastes good and can be good for the environment, too. The size and shape is perfect for reusing as a food-storage container. Applesauce and pasta sauce jars also hold leftover soup, sauce, smoothies, and more. Reduce, reuse, and recycle has never been tastier!

1. In a medium bowl, combine cornmeal, flour, and xanthan gum.

2. In a separate bowl, mix flaxseed meal with water. Add room-temperature soup and milk and stir to combine.

3. Slowly mix dry ingredients into wet.

4. Melt 1 teaspoon margarine in a skillet or griddle.

5. Drop batter to form approximately 2-inch pancakes onto hot pan.

6. When the edges firm up, flip pancakes and continue cooking on the other side.

7. While pancakes are cooking, combine salsa and drained and rinsed black beans.

8. Top each pancake with salsa.

MAKES 6 SMALL PANCAKES

Calories: 110 | Fat: 3 g | Protein: 4 g | Fiber: 3 g

Italian Eggplant

Gluten-free pasta tossed with olive oil makes a great complement to this entree.

INGREDIENTS

1 large eggplant

1 tablespoon salt

1 cup cornmeal

½ teaspoon Italian seasoning

2 tablespoons olive oil

3 cups gluten-free, casein-free pasta sauce (either homemade or jarred)

4 ounces gluten-free, casein-free soy mozzarella cheese

To Peel or Not to Peel?

It is best to keep the skin on eggplant when cooking, as that is the part of the eggplant with the greatest amount of dietary fiber. To ensure that the skin will be tender after cooking, use young, smaller eggplants rather than older eggplants, which might have tougher skin.

1. Thinly slice eggplant. (The slicing attachment on a food processor works well for this.)

2. Sprinkle eggplant slices with salt, set aside for 20 minutes, then rinse.

3. Preheat oven to 350°F.

4. Combine cornmeal, Italian seasoning, and olive oil.

5. Toss eggplant in breadcrumb mixture.

6. In a 9" × 13" lasagna pan, alternate layers of sauce and eggplant, beginning and ending with sauce.

7. Top with chopped mozzarella cheese.

8. Bake for 50–60 minutes, until cheese is melted and eggplant is tender when pierced with a fork.

SERVES 8

Calories: 221 | Fat: 7 g | Protein: 4 g | Fiber: 6 g

Lentils and Brown Rice

This iron- and fiber-rich dish can be made into a wrap-style sandwich if wrapped in a gluten-free tortilla or the Basic Crepes on page 48.

INGREDIENTS

½ cup dried lentils

1 cup short-grain brown rice

2 cups water

1 gluten-free, casein-free bouillon cube (vegetable, chicken, or beef)

⅛ teaspoon cumin

2 tablespoons gluten-free, casein-free margarine

1. Rinse and pick over lentils.

2. Combine lentils and rice in a medium saucepan.

3. Add water, bouillon, cumin, and margarine.

4. Bring to a boil.

5. Cover, and reduce heat to a simmer.

6. Cook 40 minutes.

MAKES 3 CUPS (SERVES 6)

Calories: 207 | Fat: 5 g | Protein: 7 g | Fiber: 6 g

Lentils with Spinach and Quinoa

You do not want to mix old lentils with new lentils.
The older lentils are, the longer they take to cook.
Lentils will cook unevenly if you mix old and new lentils together.

INGREDIENTS

½ cup uncooked quinoa

1 cup water

1 teaspoon oil

½ teaspoon garlic

1 cup dry lentils

Gluten-free, casein-free broth to cover lentils (vegetable, chicken, or beef)

3 cups fresh spinach

Lentil Cooking Tips

Wait! Do not add salt to the water in cooking your lentils as these might toughen the beans. Looking for another tip? Wait to add any acidic items to lentils until late in the cooking process as acidic foods make lentils take longer to cook.

1. Add quinoa and water in a microwaveable glass bowl. Cover and heat on high for 4 minutes. Remove from microwave and stir. Heat again for 2 minutes, stir, and let stand for 1 minute.

2. Pick out debris from lentils. In a medium pan, sauté garlic and oil until clear over low-medium heat. Then add lentils to pan, cover with broth, and bring to a boil for 2–3 minutes. Reduce heat to medium and cook until the lentils are tender.

3. At end of lentils cooking, add spinach to broth.

4. Drain. Combine quinoa, lentils, and spinach.

MAKES 2 CUPS (SERVES 4)

Calories: 263 | Fat: 3 g | Protein: 16 g | Fiber: 17 g

Lentil-Stuffed Green Peppers

*This entree is packed with vitamin C and protein,
and it's a crowd pleaser with family members of all ages.*

INGREDIENTS

2 cups gluten-free, casein-free
    pasta sauce (jarred or from
    page 133)

4 green bell peppers

1 recipe Lentils and Brown Rice
    (page 150)

4 slices gluten-free, casein-free
    soy mozzarella cheese

Colorful Bell Peppers

Bell peppers are available in a
rainbow of colors from green
to red to purple. All bell peppers start out green. They
change their color as they
mature. This change in color
also indicates a sweeter bell
pepper. They make a sweet
and colorful addition to salads,
stir-fries, and sauces.

1. Preheat oven to 350°F.

2. Spread ⅓ of the pasta sauce in the
   bottom of an 8-inch square pan.

3. Remove stems, seeds, and
   membranes from green peppers.

4. Stuff peppers with lentil mixture.

5. Top with cheese.

6. Spread remainder of sauce over
   peppers.

7. Bake 40 minutes.

MAKES 4 PEPPERS

Calories: 222 | Fat: 7 g | Protein: 6 g | Fiber: 7 g

Mixed-Vegetable Stir-Fry

For a heartier dish, add 1 cup of the protein of your choice and serve over brown rice.

INGREDIENTS

1 cup gluten-free, casein-free broth (vegetable, chicken, or beef)

1 tablespoon gluten-free, casein-free rice vinegar

1½ teaspoons gluten-free, casein-free soy sauce

1 tablespoon cornstarch

2 tablespoons cold water

1¼-inch piece of ginger

2 cloves of garlic

2 carrots

½ onion

2 cups broccoli florets

1 cup bok choy

1 cup cabbage

1–2 tablespoons canola oil

1. In a small bowl, combine broth, vinegar, and soysauce.

2. Dilute cornstarch in cold water and add to broth mixture.

3. Mince ginger and garlic.

4. Chop remaining vegetables.

5. In a wok or large frying pan, heat oil over high heat.

6. Add garlic and ginger, cook for 30 seconds.

7. Add carrots, onion, and broccoli. Cook for 2 minutes.

8. Add bok choy and cabbage. Cook for 1 minute.

9. Add sauce and cook for two minutes.

10. Cook until vegetables are tender, but not mushy.

MAKES 5 CUPS

Calories: 100 | Fat: 6 g | Protein: 3 g | Fiber: 2 g

Brown Rice with
Creamy Tomato Spinach Sauce

If using frozen spinach, thaw before using in this recipe.

INGREDIENTS

1 cup short-grain brown rice

½ cup gluten-free, casein-free
pasta sauce

¼ cup silken tofu

¼ cup chopped spinach

Top Rice with Your Favorite Sauce

As a change from gluten-free pastas, think about topping rice with your favorite pasta sauces. Other ideas for pasta-sauce toppables include polenta, baked potatoes, or gluten-free toast.

1. Bring 2 cups water to a boil.

2. Add rice, reduce heat, and cover. Simmer covered for 40 minutes.

3. In a food processor, combine pasta sauce, tofu, and spinach. Process until smooth.

4. Transfer sauce to a small saucepan. Heat through.

5. Stir rice into sauce.

2½ CUPS (5 SERVINGS)

Calories: 175 | Fat: 2 g | Protein: 5 g | Fiber: 2 g

Quinoa Primavera

This dish is easy to vary according to your family's tastes. You can make this dish with many different vegetables. Vary the produce options depending on the season for freshest flavor.

INGREDIENTS

1½ cups quinoa

3 cups water

1 cup frozen corn, thawed

1 red pepper, finely chopped

1 green pepper, finely chopped

1 cucumber finely chopped

Juice of 1 lemon

3 tablespoons flax oil

3 tablespoons olive oil

3 tablespoons gluten-free, casein-free rice wine vinegar

Salt to taste

1. Rinse the quinoa under cold running water until the water runs clear.

2. In a medium saucepan, place quinoa and water. Turn on medium heat and cook for 10–15 minutes or until all the water is absorbed. Fluff with fork.

3. Combine quinoa with remaining ingredients. Mix thoroughly, chill, and serve.

MAKES 8 CUPS (8 SERVINGS)

Calories: 125 | Fat: 10 g | Protein: 1 g | Fiber: 1 g

What Is Rice Wine Vinegar?

Rice wine vinegar is a popular light vinegar that is widely used in Asian cuisine. It is a vinegar made from rice wine and has a mellow and slightly sweet flavor. It is a nice addition to marinades and vinaigrette dressings, or use it to drizzle over fish before cooking to give a light flavor.

Split Pea Curry

This curry is inspired by the flavorful curries that make up the heart of Indian cooking.

INGREDIENTS

1 cup split peas

½ cup carrots

1 cup cauliflower florets

2 baking potatoes

½ cup gluten-free, casein-free tomato sauce

1½ teaspoons curry powder

1 garlic clove

1. Dice all vegetables.

2. Mince garlic.

3. Combine all ingredients in a large sauté pan or stock pot.

4. Simmer for 45 minutes to one hour, or until tender.

MAKES 5 CUPS

Calories: 255 | Fat: 1 g | Protein: 13 g | Fiber: 15 g

Making the Most of a Slow Cooker

Even parents with the best of intentions for providing home-cooked meals for their families can become overwhelmed by all of the demands that life brings. A slow cooker can be a great tool to help reduce some of that pressure. Soups, casseroles, and curries can be assembled first thing in the morning or even the night before and then cook unattended for 6–8 hours.

Tofu Spinach Lasagna

*Rice lasagna noodles will cook while the casserole
is baking and don't need to be precooked.*

INGREDIENTS

4 artichoke hearts

2 cups chopped spinach

2 tablespoons plus 2 teaspoons
olive oil, divided

1 tablespoon nutritional yeast

1 teaspoon garlic pepper

8 ounces firm tofu

2 cups gluten-free, casein-free
pasta sauce (homemade or
jarred)

6 sheets gluten-free lasagna
noodles

4 ounces gluten-free, casein-free
soy mozzarella cheese

1. Preheat oven to 350°F.

2. Finely chop artichoke hearts.

3. In a large bowl, combine artichoke
hearts, spinach, 1 tablespoon olive
oil, nutritional yeast, garlic pepper,
and tofu.

4. Spread a thin layer of pasta sauce
in the bottom of a baking pan.

5. Alternate layers of sauce, uncooked
noodles, and tofu filling.

6. Finish with sauce and top with
mozzarella.

7. Bake 40 minutes.

MAKES A 9-INCH SQUARE PAN (SERVES 9)

Calories: 197 | Fat: 8 g | Protein: 7 g | Fiber: 3 g

Vegan Cheese Options

While some soy cheese contains casein, a milk protein,
vegan cheese is completely
casein-free. Vegan cheese can
be made from a soy, rice, or
almond base. Read the label
carefully to ensure there are no
gluten-containing fillers!

Vegetable Tofu Pot Pie

Serve this warm, comforting dish with
Strawberry Applesauce (page 85) for dessert.

INGREDIENTS

2–3 potatoes

2 carrots

1 small onion

4 large mushrooms

1 cup broccoli florets

2 tablespoons olive oil

1½ cups gluten-free, casein-free
    vegetable broth

1 tablespoon nutritional yeast

1 tablespoon garlic pepper

1 tablespoon poultry seasoning

1 teaspoon dried dill

1 tablespoon cornstarch

2 tablespoons cold water

½ pound extra-firm tofu

1 frozen gluten-free pie crust or
    use Pie Crust recipe (page 55)

Nutritional Yeast

Nutritional yeast is used as a flavoring agent and as a nutritional supplement, as it provides protein and B vitamins. Some nutritional yeast is enriched with Vitamin B12. Do not confuse inactive nutritional yeast with active yeast, such as baker's yeast. Active yeasts should not be consumed raw.

1. Preheat oven to 350°F.

2. Peel potatoes and carrots and chop all vegetables into bite-size pieces.

3. Heat olive oil over medium-high heat and add potatoes, carrots, onion, and broccoli.

4. Sauté for 3–5 minutes, until slightly soft. Add mushrooms, sauté 1 more minute.

5. In a medium bowl, mix together broth, nutritional yeast, and spices.

6. Dilute cornstarch with cold water. Add to broth mixture.

7. Cut tofu into 1-inch cubes. Toss vegetables and tofu with sauce.

8. Pour into 2-quart casserole.

9. Add pie crust to top of casserole; pinch edges around top of dish.

10. Prick pie crust with a fork.

11. Bake 45–55 minutes, or until crust is golden and sauce is bubbling through holes in the crust.

MAKES 6 CUPS

Calories: 383 | Fat: 27 g | Protein: 8 g | Fiber: 4 g

Shells with Marinara Sauce

This is a wonderful homemade marinara sauce. Easy and versatile! Use this sauce in the Italian Eggplant recipe (page 149).

INGREDIENTS

1 tablespoon olive oil

1 clove garlic

2½ cups diced tomatoes (or 1 [28-ounce] can diced tomatoes, drained)

3 ounces tomato paste

1 teaspoon agave nectar

1 tablespoon fresh basil (or 1 teaspoon dried basil)

1 teaspoon dried oregano

3 cups cooked gluten-free shells

1. In a medium saucepan, heat olive oil over medium heat.

2. Add garlic, sauté for 2 minutes, until fragrant.

3. Add remaining ingredients; stir thoroughly.

4. Simmer uncovered for approximately 1 hour or until desired texture.

5. Serve sauce over whole-wheat pasta.

MAKES 3 CUPS OF SAUCE (SERVES 6)

Calories: 256 | Fat: 6 g | Protein: 8 g | Fiber: 8 g

Macaroni and Cheese

Surprisingly, giving up gluten and casein does not have to mean giving up creamy macaroni and cheese.

INGREDIENTS

8 cups (2 [32-ounce] boxes) gluten-free, casein-free broth (vegetable, chicken, or beef)

1 pound gluten-free pasta (elbow macaroni, rotini, penne, or other short shape)

1 (10-ounce) package of casein-free soy Cheddar cheese, chopped

1. In a large saucepan, bring broth to a boil.

2. Add pasta and cook according to package directions.

3. While pasta cooks, remove 2 to 3 tablespoons of broth and transfer it to another large saucepan.

4. Add chopped cheese and cook over medium heat. Stir regularly until cheese melts.

5. When pasta is done cooking, remove pasta with a slotted spoon and transfer to cheese.

6. Toss pasta with cheese until well coated.

SERVES 8

Calories: 262 | Fat: 4 g | Protein: 6 g | Fiber: 0 g

CHAPTER 10

Sandwiches and Snacks

Barbecue Chicken Pizza

Prebaking the pizza crust helps this pizza not become soggy. You can either make a homemade Cornmeal Pizza Crust (page 45) or buy a gluten- and casein-free crust at the store. Either way, bake it before adding toppings.

INGREDIENTS

3 tablespoons gluten-free, casein-free barbecue sauce

½ cup marinara sauce

1 prebaked gluten-free pizza crust

8 ounces shredded chicken

⅓ cup red onion, sliced thin

1½ cups vegan mozzarella cheese (optional)

2 tablespoons chopped cilantro (optional)

1. Preheat oven to 425°F.

2. In small bowl, combine barbecue sauce and marinara sauce. Spread on prebaked pizza crust.

3. Top pizza with chicken and red onions and cheese, if using. Bake about 15 minutes.

4. Remove from oven, sprinkle with cilantro. Serve.

YIELDS 4 SERVINGS

Calories: 267 | Fat: 12 g | Protein: 10 g | Fiber: 2 g

Cheeseless Pizzas

Vegan cheese can be an acquired taste. For people avoiding casein, it can be a great alternative to dairy cheese. For others, it just doesn't measure up. Either way, trying a pizza without cheese might seem unusual at first, but taking away the cheese allows the flavors of the toppings to shine through. So, give it a try!

Black Bean Roll-Ups

Using a 4-ounce jar of baby food carrots in this recipe makes assembling these tasty sandwiches a breeze.

INGREDIENTS

1 teaspoon olive oil

¼ cup onions, minced

1 teaspoon garlic, minced

1 (15-ounce) can black beans, drained and rinsed

4 ounces carrot puree

1 teaspoon cumin

6 corn tortillas

½ avocado, mashed

Birthday or Sleepover Party Food!

Spirals or roll-ups are typically a hit with children. You can make several different types of roll-ups and cut them into bite-size pieces. Arrange them on a plate and let your child and friends dig in! Children may be more willing to try new foods when they see other children try them . . . peer pressure in reverse!

1. Heat olive oil in skillet over medium-high heat. Add onion and garlic to skillet and sauté until clear.

2. Drain and rinse can of organic black beans.

3. Add black beans, carrot puree, and cumin to the skillet.

4. Mash with potato masher until desired consistency is reached.

5. Heat until heated through and remove from heat.

6. Heat tortillas in a dry skillet over medium heat.

7. Top each tortilla with a thin layer of bean spread and then mashed avocado.

8. Roll tortillas from end to end to make a spiral. Use a little water on the end to make them stick if needed.

9. Cut at diagonals into about 3 pieces.

YIELDS 6 TORTILLAS

Calories: 158 | Fat: 4 g | Protein: 6 g | Fiber: 8 g

Caribbean Dream Boats

Although celery is 95 percent water, this powerhouse vegetable also provides fiber, folate, and potassium. It is a great gluten- and casein-free vehicle for serving spreads and dips.

INGREDIENTS

4 washed celery stalks

1 (8-ounce) package gluten-free, casein-free soy cream cheese

1 (8-ounce) can crushed organic pineapple, drained

¼ cup shredded coconut

Tropical drink umbrellas

1. Trim celery stalks; wash and dry thoroughly.

2. Cut into 4-inch pieces.

3. Combine cream cheese and pineapple in a bowl with a spatula.

4. Spoon 2 tablespoons into celery and level with a knife.

5. Sprinkle lightly with coconut.

6. Top each with a tropical drink umbrella.

7. Cover, chill, and serve.

YIELDS 12 BOATS (12 SERVINGS)

Calories: 78 | Fat: 4 g | Protein: 1 g | Fiber: 0 g

Mix It Up!

Creativity goes a long way with children. Have fun making different arrangements with their food to tempt them to try new things. Make faces on pizzas or tortillas with vegetables, or make a "scene" with their whole plate! Let your children create art with their food, and then watch them eat it!

Creamy Spinach Mini Pizzas

Creamed spinach takes the place of traditional pizza sauce in this alternative Italian-style pie.

INGREDIENTS

Gluten-free bagel

¼ cup Creamed Spinach (page 188)

2 slices tomato

1 tablespoon gluten-free, casein-free soy Parmesan cheese (optional)

1. Cut bagel in half, and toast.

2. Spread spinach on each bagel half.

3. Top with tomato.

4. Sprinkle on Parmesan if using.

5. Broil for 2 minutes; watch to prevent burning.

MAKES 2 PIZZAS

Calories: 229 | Fat: 7 g | Protein: 8 g | Fiber: 3 g

Pizza Crust Ideas

Consider these ideas to form the base of a pizza: Gluten-free bagel, gluten-free prepared pizza crust, corn tortilla, gluten-free waffle, or gluten-free toast. With a little imagination, a pizza party is always possible.

Eggy Boats

One simple way to make the butternut squash puree is to use jarred baby food as a substitute. Baby food purees can be a healthy addition to your kitchen long after your children have outgrown baby food!

INGREDIENTS

25 snow pea pods

6 hard-boiled eggs

¼ cup gluten-free, casein-free light mayonnaise

2 tablespoons butternut squash puree

½ cup olive slices

Salt and pepper to taste

1. Wash pea pods and dry thoroughly.

2. Slice the top of the pea pod (the straight side) open so you make "pea pod boats."

3. Mash hard-boiled eggs and mix together with the light mayonnaise and butternut squash with a fork.

4. Add salt and pepper to taste.

5. Spoon 1 tablespoon into each pea pod and top with olive slices as "lifesavers."

6. Cover, chill, and serve.

YIELDS 25 BOATS (SERVING 2 BOATS)

Calories: 31 | Fat: 2 g | Protein: 2 g | Fiber: 0 g

Pizza Toast 👨‍🍳

The sky's the limit as to what other toppings you can use to customize these little pizzas. Try bell peppers, mushrooms, or even pineapple for a yummy treat.

INGREDIENTS

¼ cup gluten-free, casein-free pizza sauce

2 pieces of gluten-free, casein-free bread, toasted

2 slices gluten-free, casein-free mozzarella cheese

Easy Kid-Friendly Pizza Sauce

Combine 1 can tomato paste, ½ teaspoon garlic powder, ½ teaspoon oregano, ½ teaspoon basil, and ¾ teaspoon agave nectar, for a tasty, easy pizza sauce. Store extra sauce in an airtight container in the refrigerator.

1. Preheat oven or toaster oven to 400°F.

2. Spread half of the sauce on each piece of bread.

3. Top with cheese.

4. Cook until cheese is melted and toast is golden brown, 5–7 minutes.

MAKES 2 PIZZAS

Calories: 151 | Fat: 4 g | Protein: 5 g | Fiber: 2 g

Hummus and Mango Sandwich

This creamy, sweet sandwich provides protein,
fiber, iron, and vitamins A and C.

INGREDIENTS

2 pieces gluten-free, casein-free
bread

2 tablespoons Hummus (page
240)

¼ cup mango slices

1. Lightly toast bread.

2. Spread hummus over the surface of both pieces of bread.

3. Top one piece with mango slices.

4. Top with other piece of toast.

5. Cut sandwich in half.

MAKES 1 SANDWICH

Calories: 228 | Fat: 9 g | Protein: 4 g | Fiber: 3 g

How to Choose a Mango

When selecting a mango, two senses come into play to determine which fruit is best. First, smell the mango at the stem end. It should have a nice fruity aroma. Second, touch the mango. It should feel firm, yet yield to gentle pressure in much the same way as a peach.

Pinto Bean Burgers

Not finding gluten-free breadcrumbs? Make your own!
To make breadcrumbs, toast gluten-free bread, then let cool.
Once cool, process until crumbly.

INGREDIENTS

1 (15-ounce) can pinto beans (or 2 cups cooked)

½ medium green pepper

½ medium onion

2 garlic cloves

1 tablespoon olive oil

1 tablespoon flaxseed meal

3 tablespoons water

½ cup gluten-free, casein-free breadcrumbs

2 teaspoons olive oil

1. Drain and rinse beans. Mince green pepper, onion, and garlic.

2. In a medium skillet, heat 1 tablespoon olive oil over medium-high flame. Add vegetables and sauté until soft, approximately 3–5 minutes. Add beans and heat through.

3. Scrape bean mixture in a large bowl.

4. Mash bean mixture with a potato masher or fork.

5. Remove skillet from heat and set aside.

6. In a small bowl, combine flaxseed meal and water.

7. Combine bean mixture, flaxseed meal mixture, and breadcrumbs.

8. Form mixture into patties.

9. Add olive oil to skillet. Heat over medium flame.

10. Cook patties, turning occasionally, until browned on both sides.

MAKES 4–6 BURGERS

Calories: 187 | Fat: 7 g | Protein: 7 g | Fiber: 6 g

Pinto Bean Roll-Up

This is a quick and healthy lunch! Serve these for friends and they will not even know you are making a gluten- and casein-free lunch! These are excellent dipped in the Creamy Salsa Dip (page 244).

INGREDIENTS

1 corn tortilla

2 tablespoons pinto bean puree

2 tablespoons shredded carrots

2 tablespoons shredded cabbage

1. Warm tortilla in a dry pan over medium heat.

2. Spread pinto bean puree over the surface of the tortilla.

3. Sprinkle on carrots and cabbage.

4. Tightly roll tortilla into a tube.

5. Cut tortilla tube into three 2-inch pieces.

MAKES 1 TORTILLA

Calories: 89 | Fat: 1 g | Protein: 3 g | Fiber: 4 g

Quesadilla with Tomato

*For a change, substitute refried pinto beans
for vegan Cheddar cheese.*

INGREDIENTS

½ ripe avocado

2 corn tortillas

1 ripe tomato

¼ cup gluten-free, casein-free
    shredded Cheddar cheese

¼ cup salsa

1. Cut avocado and scrape out the insides. Mash avocado with a fork.

2. Add avocado mash on the tortilla.

3. Dice tomato and layer on top of avocado.

4. Sprinkle cheese on top of this layer and top with second tortilla

5. Heat dry skillet over medium-high flame. Place quesadilla in skillet. Heat until cheese begins to melt. Flip and cook to golden brown. Remove from heat and cut into 4 triangles.

6. Top with salsa.

YIELDS 1 QUESADILLA

Calories: 340 | Fat: 18 g | Protein: 8 g | Fiber: 12 g

Secret Beef Burgers

Serve these on your favorite gluten-free, casein-free bun! No plum puree? A handful of fresh blueberries can also have the same effects on the ground beef and boost the nutrition content of the hamburgers.

INGREDIENTS

1 pound 95 percent lean ground beef

3 tablespoons organic baby food plum puree

1 tablespoon flaxseed meal

⅓ cup onions, minced

Sea salt

Black pepper

Prunes in a Burger?

Adding prunes to your burgers may sound surprising! Prunes keep the meat very moist and add a very subtle sweet taste to the burger. Your children will not know that you are providing them a great source of antioxidants.

1. Combine ground beef, baby food, flax meal, and onions; mix lightly but thoroughly.

2. Shape loosely into four ½-inch-thick patties. Season with sea salt and pepper to taste.

3. Cook patties immediately after mixing meat mixture for best results. Heat large skillet about 2 minutes over medium heat until hot. Cook patties 10–12 minutes to desired doneness, turning once.

4. Serve burgers on whole-wheat buns with romaine or spinach lettuce, fresh tomatoes, and condiments if desired.

YIELDS 4 BURGERS

Calories: 178 | Fat: 6 g | Protein: 25 g | Fiber: 1 g

Tofu Avocado Spread

This creamy spread is rich in protein and potassium and pairs nicely with a piece of gluten-free toast, or dip your homemade corn tortilla chips in this tasty dip.

INGREDIENTS

¼ cup firm tofu

½ ripe avocado

¼ teaspoon gluten-free, casein-free soy sauce

1. Mash tofu and avocado.

2. Add soy sauce; combine well.

MAKES ½ CUP

Calories: 190 | Fat: 14 g | Protein: 9 g | Fiber: 5 g

Tofu Bites

Who needs highly processed chicken nuggets, when these tasty high-protein, gluten- and casein-free treats are so easy to make?

INGREDIENTS

1 pound tofu (firm or extra-firm)

¼ cup cornmeal (ground fine)

1 teaspoon garlic pepper

2 teaspoons olive oil

1. Preheat oven to 425°F.

2. Drain tofu and cut into 24 rectangle-shaped bites.

3. Combine cornmeal and garlic pepper in a shallow bowl.

4. Dredge each tofu piece through the cornmeal mixture.

5. Spread olive oil on a cookie sheet.

6. Bake 10 minutes or until golden brown.

MAKES 24 BITES (SERVING SIZE = 6 BITES)

Calories: 126 | Fat: 5 g | Protein: 8 g | Fiber: 1 g

Turkey Cheese Roll-Up

Pack these in a lunchbox. Many children love to pull apart wraps and sandwiches and eat all the components separately. Playing with food is a great way for children to explore and accept new tastes and textures!

INGREDIENTS

6 corn tortillas

¾ cup gluten-free, casein-free soy cream cheese

12 ounces gluten-free, casein-free oven-roasted turkey, sliced

2 cups red cabbage, shredded

1 cucumber, sliced

2 carrots, shredded

Rice wine vinegar

1. Warm each tortilla in a dry skillet over medium heat.

2. Top each one with 2 tablespoons of cream cheese and spread over all tortilla.

3. Top with 3 ounces of turkey, ⅓ cup shredded cabbage, slices of cucumber, and shredded carrots.

4. Sprinkle rice wine vinegar to taste.

5. Roll up tortilla and slice across each tortilla to make 2 smaller wraps.

YIELDS 6 TORTILLAS

Calories: 245 | Fat: 8 g | Protein: 18 g | Fiber: 3 g

Veggie Roll-Up

This wrap-style sandwich combines textures in a really appealing way.

INGREDIENTS

2 corn tortillas

4 tablespoons Tofu Avocado
Spread (page 173)

2 tablespoons chopped tomato

2 tablespoons minced red pepper

2 tablespoons chopped cucumber

1. Spread Tofu Avocado Spread across surface of the tortilla.

2. Sprinkle on vegetables.

3. Tightly roll tortilla into a tube.

4. Cut the tube in half.

YIELDS 2 TORTILLAS

Calories: 234 | Fat: 10 g | Protein: 8 g | Fiber: 7 g

Zucchini Yacht 🍳

This recipe makes a great dish for a group.
Serve this with Eggy Boats on page 166 and Caribbean Dream Boats
on page 164 and have a boat parade for your children!

Serve this with Eggy Boats on page 166 and Caribbean Dream Boats on page 164

INGREDIENTS

1 zucchini

1 summer yellow squash, chopped

¼ red onion, chopped

1 ripe mango

½ cup finely chopped cilantro

2 tablespoons gluten-free, casein-free red wine vinegar

1 tablespoon olive oil

Zucchini Vessels

Hollowed-out zucchinis make great vessels to hold different foods. Fill the zucchini with egg salad, chicken salad, or a fruit salad. Nutritionally, your children will get small amounts of folate, potassium, vitamin A, and manganese when eating zucchini.

1. Slice zucchini lengthwise forming 2 long boats.

2. Scrape out shallow middle of the zucchini to form the hull of the boat.

3. Combine yellow squash, onion, mango, and cilantro and mix with red wine vinegar, and olive oil until coated thoroughly.

4. Fill the zucchini boats with this filling.

5. Serve on a slice of romaine lettuce for the "water."

YIELDS 2 YACHTS

Calories: 169 | Fat: 7 g | Protein: 3 g | Fiber: 4 g

Spicy Meatballs

Meatballs always have bread as a filler and outside coating. Here, we use ground potato chips. The eggs will hold the balls together, and the ground chips taste wonderful.

INGREDIENTS

1 pound 90 percent fat ground beef

2 eggs

2 cloves garlic, minced

1 teaspoon dried oregano

½ teaspoon cinnamon

½ teaspoon fennel seeds

½ cup finely grated gluten-free, casein-free Parmesan cheese

Salt and pepper to taste

2 cups crushed low-salt potato chips, divided

Light oil, such as canola, for frying

1. In a large bowl, mix all ingredients except 1 cup of the chip crumbs and the cooking oil.

2. Place a large sheet of waxed paper on the counter. Sprinkle remaining cup of chip crumbs on it.

3. Form meatballs, roll in crumbs, and fry them in oil until well browned. Drain on paper towels and then either refrigerate, freeze, or serve with the marinara sauce of your choice.

MAKES 10 TO 12 MEATBALLS

Calories: 303 | Fat: 19 g | Protein: 12 g | Fiber: 2 g

Spicy Meatballs

You can add flavor to your meatballs by grinding up some sweet or hot Italian sausage and mixing it with the beef. A truly great Italian sausage has aromatics like garlic, and herbs and spices such as anise seeds.

Curried Chicken

This whole concept is very Middle Eastern.
This is to be stuffed in the Basic Crepes on page 48.

INGREDIENTS

1 recipe Basic Crepes (page 48)

½ pound chicken breast, poached for 10 minutes, or leftover cooked chicken, minced

½ cup gluten-free, casein-free plain soy yogurt

2 teaspoons curry powder, or to taste

¼ cup mango chutney

1. Stack the crepes with waxed paper between them. Mix together the chicken, curry powder, and chutney. Place a spoonful of the chicken curry mixture on a quarter section of each crepe.

2. Fold in quarters. Place on a platter and serve.

SERVES 8

Calories: 89 | Fat: 3 g | Protein: 9 g | Fiber: 0 g

Fried Polenta Squares with Salsa

Make the polenta a day in advance,
then refrigerate it until just before the party.

INGREDIENTS

6½ cups water

2 tablespoons salt

2 cups yellow cornmeal

2–4 ounces gluten-free, casein-free margarine

2 tablespoons dried herbs or 1 tablespoon each fresh: basil, rosemary, and parsley

½ cup gluten-free, casein-free Parmesan cheese

Freshly ground black pepper to taste

4–6 tablespoons canola oil, for frying

1 (8-ounce) jar of your favorite salsa or homemade Guacamole (page 239) for dipping

1. Bring the water to a boil.

2. Add salt, and using your hand, drop the cornmeal into the boiling water, letting it slip slowly between your fingers to make a very slim stream. You should be able to see each grain. Do not dump the cornmeal into the water or you will get a mass of glue.

3. Stir constantly while adding the cornmeal. Reduce heat to a simmer and keep stirring for about 20 minutes as it thickens.

4. Stir in the margarine, herbs, Parmesan cheese, and pepper. Spread in a 9" × 13" glass pan that has been prepared with nonstick spray.

5. Chill for 3 hours or overnight. Cut into squares and fry until golden brown over medium heat in oil. If you are having an outdoor party, you can grill the squares over low flame for a smoky flavor. Serve with salsa or Guacamole.

MAKES 12 SQUARES

Calories: 143 | Fat: 10 g | Protein: 1 g | Fiber: 1 g

Homemade Potato Chips

These are just too good and will be grabbed fast,
so plan to make extra.

INGREDIENTS

4 large Yukon Gold potatoes

1 cup canola oil

Salt to taste

1. Peel and slice the potatoes. The best way to slice these chips is with a mandolin or the slicing blade on your food processor.

2. Place 2 inches of oil in the fryer. Heat the oil to 340°F and watch the temperature throughout the cooking time.

3. Carefully add potato slices, a few at a time, to hot oil. Remove when golden and drain on brown paper bags or paper towels. Sprinkle with salt. Serve hot or warm. (For a variation, mix 2 teaspoons chili powder with 2 teaspoons salt and sprinkle on the chips as they cool.)

MAKES ABOUT 50 CHIPS (SERVING = 10 CHIPS)

Calories: 312 | Fat: 23 g | Protein: 3 g | Fiber: 3 g

CHAPTER 11

Vegetable Sides

Vegetable Baked Risotto

*This delicious dish delivers protein, iron,
fiber, and a variety of vitamins.*

INGREDIENTS

3 cups gluten-free, casein-free
   vegetable broth

½ cup green beans

1 cup Arborio rice

1 cup broccoli florets

1 small zucchini

1 garlic clove

1 cup cooked great northern
   beans

1 teaspoon dried basil

1 teaspoon dried oregano

1. Preheat oven to 325°F.

2. Bring broth to a boil.

3. Drain and rinse green beans and
   rinse rice.

4. Trim ends from green beans; cut
   into 1-inch pieces.

5. Divide broccoli into small florets,
   and coarsely chop zucchini.

6. Mince garlic.

7. Drain and rinse great northern
   beans.

8. Combine all ingredients in a
   covered casserole. Bake 1 hour.

MAKES 4½ CUPS (SERVES 6)

Calories: 200 | Fat: 1 g | Protein: 7 g | Fiber: 5 g

Apple-Roasted Carrots

If your child is a reluctant utensil user, carrot slices make a good finger food. You can also use these for dips!

INGREDIENTS

4 large carrots

¼ cup apple juice concentrate

1. Peel and thinly slice carrots.

2. Preheat oven to 450°F.

3. Toss carrots with apple juice concentrate.

4. Bake 10–12 minutes, or until carrots are tender.

MAKES ¾ CUP

Calories: 118 | Fat: 0 g | Protein: 1 g | Fiber: 2 g

Hawaiian Sweet Potatoes

Roasting the sweet potatoes with the pineapple gives this dish a festive air without any added sugar.

INGREDIENTS

1 large sweet potato

1 cup chopped pineapple

The World-Traveling Pineapple

Although pineapples are native to Paraguay and Brazil, they made their way around the world on sailing vessels. Sailors ate them to prevent scurvy. The same vitamin C that helped sailors helps keep today's little ones healthy.

1. Preheat oven to 375°F.

2. Wash sweet potato and cut into wedges lengthwise.

3. Arrange sweet potato wedges in a small baking dish.

4. Cover sweet potatoes with pineapple pieces and juice.

5. Bake 45–55 minutes, or until sweet potatoes are very tender.

MAKES 2 CUPS (SERVES 2)

Calories: 97 | Fat: 0 g | Protein: 1 g | Fiber: 3 g

Cauliflower and Potato Mash

Here is a twist on mashed potatoes! Add other items to these "mashed potatoes" based on your child's taste.
Try adding peas to this mash for a little more texture.

INGREDIENTS

2 large potatoes, chopped

1 head of cauliflower, cut into florets

1 cup gluten-free, casein-free soy milk

1 tablespoon gluten-free, casein-free margarine

Are There Different Colors of Cauliflower?

Yes, there are! There is a purple cauliflower that contains the antioxidant anthocyanin, which is also in red wine and cabbage. There is green cauliflower, which is called broccoflower. And there is orange cauliflower, which contains 25 times more vitamin A than white cauliflower . . . it competes well with carrots!

1. Place potatoes in a medium pot and cover with water. Boil the potatoes for 10 minutes until soft, drain, and return to pot.

2. Steam the cauliflower until tender, drain, and add to pot with potatoes.

3. Add soy milk and margarine to potatoes and cauliflower.

4. Mash with a potato masher or use a beater to get a thinner puree.

YIELDS 5 CUPS

Calories: 126 | Fat: 3 g | Protein: 5 g | Fiber: 5 g

Creamed Spinach

*Serve this creamed spinach on a baked potato
for a more-filling dish.*

INGREDIENTS

1 bunch spinach

½ gluten-free dinner roll

2 tablespoons olive oil

1 clove garlic

2 tablespoons gluten-free all-
purpose flour

½ teaspoon salt

¼ teaspoon pepper

2–4 tablespoons gluten-free,
casein-free soy milk

Toppings for a Baked Potato

When you change to a casein-free diet, some old favorites have to change, too. What can you put on a baked potato when butter is not an option? Trans-fat-free vegan buttery spread is a great replacement for butter, but other ideas can turn that plain potato into a hearty meal. This creamed spinach, chili, or even pasta sauce all help potatoes take center stage on the dinner plate. Olive oil is also a tasty condiment for a baked potato, especially when dining out.

1. Thoroughly wash spinach and remove stems.

2. Roughly chop spinach.

3. Wilt spinach in a dry skillet over medium heat.

4. Combine wilted spinach with roll in a food processor.

5. Process until finely chopped.

6. Heat olive oil over medium flame.

7. Sauté minced garlic until fragrant.

8. Add flour, then salt and pepper.

9. Add 2 tablespoons soy milk.

10. Add spinach mixture.

11. Add more soy milk until desired consistency.

12. Heat through.

SERVES 3

Calories: 141 | Fat: 10 g | Protein: 4 g | Fiber: 3 g

Frosted Cauliflower

For a more striking presentation, this can be made with the whole head intact and then divided into florets when serving.

INGREDIENTS

1 head cauliflower

¼ cup gluten-free, casein-free plain soy yogurt

2 tablespoons prepared yellow mustard

1 teaspoon agave nectar

½ cup shredded gluten-free, casein-free soy Cheddar cheese

1. Preheat oven to 350°F.

2. Bring a large pot of water to a boil.

3. Cut cauliflower into florets.

4. Drop florets into boiling water, cook for 1–2 minutes. Drain and rinse under cold water.

5. In a small bowl, mix together yogurt, mustard, and agave nectar.

6. Toss cauliflower in sauce.

7. Transfer to 1½ quart casserole dish, cover with cheese.

8. Bake, uncovered, for 20–25 minutes, or until cheese is melted.

MAKES 3 CUPS (4 SERVINGS)

Calories: 93 | Fat: 2 g | Protein: 5 g | Fiber: 4 g

Orange Beets

How to boil your own beets: First, cut off the tops and 1 inch of stem. Wash beets but do not peel. Place in pot with boiling water and cook for ½ to 2 hours. The skins slip off easily when done.

INGREDIENTS

1 (8-ounce) package peeled and steamed ready-to-eat baby beets

1 can (6-ounce) mandarin oranges

1 fresh apple, cut into slices

¼ cup canola oil

3 tablespoons orange juice

1 tablespoon lemon juice

1 teaspoon orange zest

1. Slice beets into tiny small slices.

2. In large mixing bowl, combine beets with mandarin oranges and apples.

3. In a small bowl, combine oil, orange juice, and lemon juice.

4. Toss dressing over fruit and chill. Serve.

MAKES 4 CUPS

Calories: 190 | Fat: 14 g | Protein: 1 g | Fiber: 2 g

Beets Not Your Child's Favorite Food?

It can take a while for your child to develop a taste for beets. Beets have one of the highest natural sugar contents of any vegetable, so they are great for roasting. Try roasting beets to bring out a sweeter flavor that might tempt your child. You can also try canned beets and see if they will accept them.

Grilled Summer Vegetables

Grill vegetables on the top rack of the grill. Don't choose vegetables with a high water content, like cucumbers. They will not grill well. Stick to heartier vegetables and fruits to grill.

INGREDIENTS

1 head broccoli, trimmed into florets

1 yellow summer squash, sliced

3 fresh ripe tomatoes, cut into wedges

1 red onion, sliced

½ cup gluten-free, casein-free Italian dressing

¼ teaspoon sea salt

1. Combine all ingredients.

2. Wrap in aluminum foil.

3. Place on top rack of hot grill for 5–7 minutes or until vegetables are tender.

4. Remove from heat and transfer to serving bowl.

YIELDS 4 CUPS

Calories: 156 | Fat: 9 g | Protein: 5 g | Fiber: 5 g

Check the Label on Your Salad Dressing

Many Italian dressings are basically oil, vinegar, spices, and sweeteners. Always check the ingredients, though, to ensure that there isn't any cheese or gluten (barley malt, in particular) in the brand you're using. Remember to check the label every time you buy even a trusted brand, because ingredients can change with no notice.

Herbed Broccoli

*Save the stalks from the broccoli
and use them to make vegetable broth.*

INGREDIENTS

Large head of broccoli

¼ cup vegetable broth

¼ teaspoon basil, dried

¼ teaspoon oregano, dried

⅛ teaspoon thyme, dried

⅛ teaspoon savory, dried

1. Cut bite-size florets from the head of broccoli.

2. Toss florets with broth and herbs.

3. Steam in microwave 3 minutes or in a steamer basket until desired tenderness.

MAKES 2½ CUPS

Calories: 105 | Fat: 1 g | Protein: 9 g | Fiber: 8 g

Honeyed Carrots

*This is another great way to provide carrots
with a little extra sweetness.*

INGREDIENTS

1 pound carrot coins, steamed

1 tablespoon gluten-free, casein-
free margarine

2 tablespoons wildflower honey

1 tablespoon agave nectar

1 tablespoon lemon or lime juice

1. Steam carrot coins in the microwave until tender.

2. In medium saucepan over medium heat, melt margarine.

3. In small bowl, combine honey, agave nectar, and lemon or lime juice.

4. Add carrots and honey mixture to saucepan with margarine.

5. Heat through and mix until coated with honey mixture.

6. Remove with slotted spoon and serve. Sprinkle with salt to taste.

YIELDS 1 POUND OF CARROTS (8 SERVINGS)

Calories: 57 | Fat: 23 g | Protein: 0 g | Fiber: 2 g

Maple Acorn Squash

Cooking acorn squash in a water bath results in an extremely tender side dish.

INGREDIENTS

1 acorn squash

2 tablespoons pure maple syrup

1. Preheat oven to 375°F.

2. Cut squash in half; scoop out seeds and discard.

3. Place squash cut-side down in a square baking pan.

4. Fill with water until it is 1–2 inches deep.

5. Bake 45 minutes or until flesh is very tender.

6. Pour off water, turn squash cut-side up and pour 1 tablespoon maple syrup into each half.

7. Turn oven to broiler setting. Broil 2 minutes. Serve.

MAKES 2 HALVES

Calories: 80 | Fat: 0 g | Protein: 1 g | Fiber: 1 g

Mashed Potatoes and Parsnips

Yukon Gold potatoes have a rich flavor,
creamy texture, and beautiful color.

INGREDIENTS

4 Yukon Gold potatoes

2 parsnips

1 tablespoon olive oil

¼ teaspoon salt, optional

Parsnips, a Late-Fall Treat

Parsnips look very similar to white carrots. Because they are at their sweetest after having been exposed to cold temperatures, they are best in the late fall or early winter. Cook them in the same way as carrots for great-tasting results.

1. Peel potatoes and parsnips.

2. Roughly chop vegetables and place in a medium saucepan.

3. Cover with water.

4. Bring to a boil, then reduce heat to a simmer.

5. Cook until vegetables are tender, approximately 10–15 minutes, depending on size of chopped pieces.

6. Drain, reserving cooking liquid.

7. Return vegetables to pot, mash with a potato masher or fork; stir in olive oil and salt if using.

8. Add reserved cooking water, one tablespoon at a time, until mash is the desired consistency.

MAKES 3 CUPS (6 SERVNGS)

Calories: 223 | Fat: 3 g | Protein: 5 g | Fiber: 8 g

Mashed "Sweet" Potatoes

*If part of your sweet potato is bad, you cannot just remove
the bad part and use the rest of the potato.
If part of it is bad, you have to get rid of the whole potato!*

INGREDIENTS

4 sweet potatoes, peeled

¼ cup gluten-free, casein-free margarine

¼ cup honey

¼ cup light agave nectar

½ cup gluten-free, casein-free soy milk

1. Peel potatoes and cube them.

2. Bring pot of water to a boil. Place potatoes in boiling water and boil for about 20 minutes.

3. Drain potatoes and place in mixing bowl.

4. Add margarine, honey, and light agave nectar, mix well.

5. Add soy milk to reach desired texture.

YIELDS 4 CUPS (8 SERVINGS)

Calories: 160 | Fat: 6 g | Protein: 1 g | Fiber: 2 g

"Milk" Versus "Drink"

Most commercially available cows' milk substitutes use the word "milk" in their names, although they are not the milk produced by a lactating animal. Some people prefer to call such a beverage a "drink" as opposed to "milk" to avoid confusing the child who knows she cannot drink cows' milk. Whatever you call your milk alternative of choice, make sure that your child knows the difference between what's okay to drink and cows' milk, which is not okay on a casein-free diet.

Roasted Potato Rounds

Baking potatoes or Yukon Gold potatoes
can be substituted for red potatoes.

INGREDIENTS

3 large red potatoes

2 tablespoons olive oil

Sprinkling of sea salt

Acceptable "Junk" Food

It is not unusual for some children with autism to be extremely limited in their food choices. What if fries and other not-so-healthy choices are among the very few options that your child will eat? Try to offer a healthier version of the favored food. For example, roasted potato rounds (or cut into fry shapes) can provide a healthy alternative to French fries. If your child won't try them when first served, try again in the future.

1. Preheat oven to 475°F.

2. Wash and thinly slice potatoes.

3. Spread 1 tablespoon olive oil on baking sheet.

4. Spread potato slices on top of oil.

5. Top with remaining oil and salt.

6. Bake 13–15 minutes, until soft and golden.

MAKES 24 ROUNDS (4 SERVINGS)

Calories: 158 | Fat: 7 g | Protein: 3 g | Fiber: 3 g

Potato Smash Up

You can also leave the skin on the russet potatoes for a different texture in your potatoes. Both russet and new potatoes taste nice with the skin on. Sweet potato skin does not usually taste good in recipes.

INGREDIENTS

2 sweet potatoes

2 russet potatoes

1½ cups butternut squash

¼ cup gluten-free, casein-free margarine

½–1 cup gluten-free, casein-free soy milk

1. Peel potatoes and squash and cube them into pieces of about the same size.

2. Bring pot of water to a boil. Place potatoes and squash in boiling water and boil for about 20 minutes.

3. Drain potatoes and squash and place in mixing bowl.

4. Add margarine and smash with a potato masher or hand mixer.

5. Add soy milk to reach desired texture.

YIELDS 6 CUPS (6 SERVINGS)

Calories: 191 | Fat: 8 g | Protein: 3 g | Fiber: 4 g

Roasted Carrots

Careful preparation is needed in this dish to ensure that small children aren't at risk for choking. Roast the carrots so they are soft and easily chewed. Cut the ingredients into pieces that are smaller than the child's windpipe.

INGREDIENTS

8 ounces baby carrots, cut into thirds

1 tablespoon gluten-free, casein-free margarine, melted

1 tablespoon agave nectar

⅛ teaspoon cinnamon

1 pound red seedless grapes, cut in quarters

1 pear, sliced

Roasting Fruit in the Oven?

Roasting fruits is a wonderful way to bring out the sweetness in your fruit. Winter fruits tend to roast better than summer fruits. Pears, apples, and oranges all roast wonderfully. Lightly toss them with olive oil and a little sea salt and roast them in a 450–500°F oven to bring out their roasted taste!

1. Preheat oven to 450°F.

2. In the microwave, steam carrots until slightly tender.

3. In separate bowl, melt margarine and combine with cinnamon and agave nectar.

4. Remove carrots from microwave. In medium bowl combine all ingredients.

5. Spread out on a baking sheet and roast in preheated oven for 10–15 minutes or until tender.

MAKES 1½ POUNDS (10 SERVINGS)

Calories: 60 | Fat: 1 g | Protein: 1 g | Fiber: 2 g

Roasted Winter Vegetables

This method works well for any root vegetable, including turnips, rutabagas, and beets.

INGREDIENTS

1 large sweet potato

1 small butternut squash

2 medium parsnips

2 tablespoons olive oil

Salt and pepper to taste

Roasted Squash Seeds

If you enjoy roasting pumpkin seeds on Halloween, you will probably enjoy snacking on high-protein roasted squash seeds all year long. Clean the stringy part of the squash off the seeds, spread on a lightly oiled baking sheet, and sprinkle with salt. Bake at 350°F for approximately 15 minutes, watching to ensure that they don't burn. Store in a sealed jar.

1. Preheat oven to 425°F.

2. Peel all vegetables and cut into chunks. (Remove seeds from squash before cutting.)

3. Toss in olive oil and salt and pepper, if using.

4. Spread in a single layer on a cookie sheet.

5. Bake until tender and sweet, approximately 20 minutes.

MAKES 6 CUPS (SERVES 6)

Calories: 102 | Fat: 5 g | Protein: 1 g | Fiber: 3 g

Spaghetti Squash with Italian Herbs

Spaghetti squash is also delicious when it is served with a tomato sauce, like the one in the recipe for Shells with Marinara Sauce (page 159).

INGREDIENTS

1 spaghetti squash

2 tablespoons olive oil

1 garlic clove

1 teaspoon dried basil

1 teaspoon dried oregano

¼ cup gluten-free, casein-free Parmesan cheese

Amazing Gluten-Free, Casein-Free, All-Natural Spaghetti Squash!

Spaghetti squash works as a pasta stand-in with almost any pasta sauce. Try pestos, tomato-based sauces, or top a serving of spaghetti squash and olive oil with chili.

1. Preheat oven to 350°F.

2. Pierce squash with a fork in several places.

3. Bake 1½ hours (1 hour for a small squash).

4. Cut in half and remove seeds.

5. Scrape flesh with the tines of a fork to form spaghetti-type threads.

6. Heat olive oil over medium flame.

7. Add minced garlic and herbs. Cook 2 minutes or until garlic is golden, but not brown.

8. Toss "spaghetti" with oil and herbs. Top with Parmesan cheese if using.

MAKES 4–6 CUPS

Calories: 86 | Fat: 6 g | Protein: 1 g | Fiber: 0 g

Sweet Potato Fries

Timesaver tip: Purchase sweet potatoes already peeled and ready to cook! If you use this technique with frozen potatoes, it will help them remain crispy.

INGREDIENTS

4 sweet potatoes, peeled and cut into matchsticks

Large pot of boiling water

Large bowl of ice water

2 egg whites

⅛ teaspoon garlic powder

Why So Many Steps for Sweet Potato Fries?

The moisture content of sweet potatoes is very high and often makes for very soggy fries. The blanching and parchment paper all help to prevent soggy fries. One last tip: Make sure not to crowd the baking sheet with too many potatoes. If they are too close, they steam each other and then become soggy.

1. Preheat oven to 450°F.

2. Blanch the potatoes: Bring a large pot of water to a boil. Place potatoes in and cook for 5 minutes. Drain and immediately plunge into bowl of ice water.

3. Dry the potatoes well. Combine egg whites and garlic powder.

4. Toss potatoes with egg white mixture.

5. Line baking sheet with parchment paper and bake for 14 minutes.

6. Turn once about 7 minutes into cooking.

YIELDS 4 CUPS

Calories: 120 | Fat: 0 g | Protein: 4 g | Fiber: 4 g

Veggie Stuffing

To make breadcrumbs, toast 8 pieces of gluten-free bread in a 200°F oven for 10–15 minutes, or until relatively dried out. Chop toasted bread into ½-inch pieces.

INGREDIENTS

2 tablespoons gluten-free, casein-free margarine

2 carrots, peeled and coarsely chopped

1 celery stalk, coarsely chopped

1 onion, finely chopped

1 cup chopped button mushrooms

¼ teaspoon black pepper

½ teaspoon gluten-free, casein-free poultry seasoning

4 cups gluten-free, casein-free breadcrumbs

2 cups gluten-free, casein-free broth (vegetable, chicken, or beef)

1. Preheat oven to 350°F.

2. Grease a 2-quart casserole.

3. Melt margarine over a medium flame.

4. Sauté vegetables until soft.

5. Add seasonings, sauté another 2–3 minutes.

6. Add breadcrumbs, and toss to mix.

7. Add broth, and toss to mix.

8. Spread mixture in casserole.

9. Bake for 35–45 minutes. Cook longer for drier stuffing.

MAKES 6 CUPS

Calories: 95 | Fat: 1 g | Protein: 3 g | Fiber: 3 g

Gluten-Free Breads

There are a wide range of breads that are gluten-free and casein-free available at your local natural foods store. Choices range from brown rice, tapioca, or mixed-grain breads. Experiment with different options to find the ones that you like best. Most of these breads taste best when they are toasted and eaten right away.

Stuffing for Roasted Turkey

Make your own gluten-free cornbread for stuffing a day or two before, cube, and place in the refrigerator in a plastic bag until ready to use.

INGREDIENTS

1 onion, finely chopped

4 stalks celery with tops, finely chopped

4 tablespoons olive oil

1 pound bulk gluten-free, casein-free breakfast sausage

10 cups cubed gluten-free, casein-free bread or gluten-free, casein-free cornbread

1 cup gluten-free, casein-free margarine, melted with ½ cup water

2 teaspoons dried thyme

10 fresh sage leaves, minced, or 2 tablespoons dried

2 large tart apples, peeled, cored, and chopped

Salt and pepper to taste

1. In a large frying pan, sauté the onion and celery in the olive oil. Add the sausage and break up with a wooden spoon. Cook until sausage is done and vegetables are tender. Place in a very large bowl.

2. Add the rest of the ingredients to the bowl. Mix the ingredients well with your hands covered in large plastic bags. Stuff your turkey with this mixture.

MAKES ENOUGH STUFFING FOR 1 TURKEY (15 SERVINGS)

Calories: 332 | Fat: 29 g | Protein: 6 g | Fiber: 1 g

Vary Your Stuffing

You can make this stuffing really come alive with extra ingredients such as fresh oysters, shucked and chopped; dried cranberries; or coarsely chopped pecans or walnuts.

Pumpkin Risotto

This colorful dish makes a lovely meal when paired with a protein such as beans or meat, and a green salad or green vegetable. It also makes a great addition to a Thanksgiving feast!

INGREDIENTS

1 tablespoon olive oil

1 tablespoon gluten-free, casein-free margarine

1 tablespoon fresh sage

1 garlic clove

¼ cup chopped onion

1 cup Arborio rice

1 cup canned pumpkin

3 cups gluten-free, casein-free vegetable broth

1. Preheat oven to 350°F.

2. In a small skillet, heat olive oil and margarine over medium-high heat.

3. When oil mixture is sizzling, add sage and minced garlic. Sauté 1 minute.

4. Transfer herb mixture to a 3-quart casserole.

5. Add remaining ingredients and cover.

6. Bake 1 hour. Stir before serving.

MAKES 5 CUPS (10 SERVINGS)

Calories: 124 | Fat: 3 g | Protein: 2 g | Fiber: 2 g

Winter Squash

Pumpkin is a gourd-style squash, similar to acorn squash or butternut squash. They can be interchanged for good results in many recipes.

Mixed Vegetable Kabobs

Serve these kabobs with quinoa, beans, and some sliced melon for a complete summertime meal.

INGREDIENTS

1 carrot

1 red bell pepper

4 mushrooms

1 small zucchini

1 green bell pepper

2 tablespoons olive oil

Salt and pepper to taste

1. Peel carrot, and chop all vegetables into 1½ -inch pieces.

2. Toss with olive oil and salt and pepper, if using.

3. Grill or broil, until the vegetables are tender, turning once.

MAKES 2 KABOBS

Calories: 202 | Fat: 14 g | Protein: 4 g | Fiber: 5 g

Alternative Pastas

At many well-stocked grocery stores there are a variety of pastas available made from gluten-free grains. These options run the gamut from brown rice to quinoa or corn. Try them with tomato-based sauces, in soups, or tossed with olive oil and pepper and fresh herbs.

CHAPTER 12

Desserts

Blueberry Sorbet

This all-fruit sorbet is a great way to provide vitamin C in a fun way.

INGREDIENTS

1½ cup blueberries

½ cup lemonade

2 tablespoons apple juice
   concentrate

1. Combine all ingredients in a blender or food processor, and puree until smooth.

2. Pour into a freezer-safe container.

3. Freeze for 2 hours, then fluff with a fork.

4. Return to freezer.

5. Continue fluffing every 1½–2 hours until serving.

MAKES 2¼ CUPS (4 SERVINGS)

Calories: 56 | Fat: 0 g | Protein: 0 g | Fiber: 1 g

Broiled Pineapple
and Vanilla Frozen Yogurt

This "dessert" provides protein, calcium, and vitamin C.

INGREDIENTS

8 ounces gluten-free, casein-free vanilla soy yogurt

1 cup pineapple chunks

1. Transfer yogurt to a freezer-safe container.

2. Freeze for 1 hour, stir, and return to freezer.

3. Preheat oven to broiler setting.

4. Broil pineapple until slightly browned, approximately 10 minutes.

5. If yogurt is frozen too hard, let sit on counter for a few minutes to soften. Stir in pineapple chunks before serving.

MAKES 2 CUPS

Calories: 37 | Fat: 2 g | Protein: 5 g | Fiber: 2 g

Sweet Potato Pie

This pie has a soft texture.
If you prefer a firmer pie, refrigerate before serving.

INGREDIENTS

1 Pie Crust (page 55)

2 cups sweet potato puree

½ cup pure maple syrup

½ teaspoon nutmeg

¼ teaspoon ginger

1 teaspoon gluten-free vanilla

2 tablespoons flaxseed meal

4 tablespoons water

1. Preheat oven to 425°F.

2. Prebake pie crust for 5 minutes.

3. In a medium bowl, combine sweet potato puree, syrup, nutmeg, ginger, and vanilla.

4. In a small bowl, combine flaxseed and water. Let sit 3–4 minutes.

5. Mix flaxseed mixture into sweet potato mixture.

6. Pour filling into pie crust.

7. Bake for 15 minutes.

8. Reduce heat to 350°F, and bake for another 40–45 minutes.

9. Cool completely before serving.

SERVES 9

Calories: 236 | Fat: 15 g | Protein: 3 g | Fiber: 2 g

Apple Pie

*Top warm slices of this pie with vanilla soy ice cream
for an all-American treat.*

INGREDIENTS

2 pie crusts (either store-bought
   or from recipe on page 55)

6 Granny Smith apples

1 teaspoon cinnamon

¼ teaspoon allspice

½ cup packed light brown sugar

2 tablespoons tapioca flour

1. Preheat oven to 375°F.

2. Prebake 1 crust for 5 minutes.

3. Peel and thinly slice apples.

4. Toss apple slices with cinnamon, allspice, brown sugar, and tapioca flour.

5. Fill pie crust with apple slices.

6. Top pie with second crust.

7. Pierce top of pie crust with a knife to create steam vents.

8. Bake 40 minutes.

SERVES 9

Calories: 427 | Fat: 28 g | Protein: 4 g | Fiber: 5 g

Vanilla Cupcakes

These cupcakes have a light, fluffy texture and pair well with either Chocolate Frosting (page 214) or Vanilla Frosting (page 215).

INGREDIENTS

2 cups gluten-free all-purpose flour

1 teaspoon xanthan gum

1 cup turbinado sugar

1 tablespoon plus ½ teaspoon baking powder, divided

½ teaspoon salt

8 tablespoons gluten-free, casein-free margarine

1 cup gluten-free, casein-free soy milk

1 teaspoon apple cider vinegar

2 teaspoons gluten-free vanilla

½ cup applesauce

1. Oil a standard muffin pan.

2. In a medium bowl, combine flour, xanthan gum, sugar, 1 tablespoon baking powder, and salt.

3. In a small saucepan, combine margarine and soy milk over medium heat.

4. Stir until margarine is melted.

5. Stir vinegar and vanilla into soy milk mixture.

6. In a small bowl, combine applesauce with ½ teaspoon baking powder.

7. Mix applesauce mixture into soy milk mixture.

8. Combine wet ingredients and dry ingredients. Stir just until mixed.

9. Bake 15–18 minutes, or until a toothpick inserted into the center of a cupcake comes out clean.

MAKES 12 CUPCAKES

Calories: 219 | Fat: 8 g | Protein: 2 g | Fiber: 2 g

Chocolate Cupcakes

*If you don't have turbinado sugar,
you can substitute granulated sugar.*

INGREDIENTS

2 cups gluten-free all-purpose
flour

1 teaspoon xanthan gum

1 cup turbinado sugar

1 tablespoon plus ½ teaspoon
baking powder, divided

½ teaspoon salt

¼ cup cocoa

8 tablespoons (½ cup) gluten-free,
casein-free margarine

1 cup gluten-free, casein-free soy
milk

½ cup applesauce

1 teaspoon apple cider vinegar

2 teaspoons gluten-free vanilla

1. Preheat oven to 375°F.

2. In a large bowl, combine flour,
   xanthan gum, sugar, salt, 1
   tablespoon baking powder, and
   cocoa.

3. In a small saucepan, combine
   margarine and soy milk over medium-
   low heat. Stir until margarine is
   melted, then remove from heat.

4. In a small bowl, combine
   applesauce with ½ teaspoon of
   baking powder.

5. Mix vinegar and vanilla in with
   applesauce mixture. Mix soy milk
   mixture into applesauce mixture.

6. Mix wet ingredients into dry
   ingredients.

7. Spoon batter into well-oiled
   standard muffin pan (or use muffin
   papers).

8. Bake 15–18 minutes, or until a
   toothpick inserted into the center
   of a cupcake comes out clean.

MAKES 12 CUPCAKES

Calories: 223 | Fat: 9 g | Protein: 3 g | Fiber: 3 g

Chocolate Frosting

Chocolate frosting is the perfect topping for either Vanilla Cupcakes (page 212) or Chocolate Cupcakes (page 213).

INGREDIENTS

2 tablespoons gluten-free, casein-free shortening

2 tablespoons gluten-free, casein-free margarine

2 teaspoons gluten-free vanilla

2–3 tablespoons gluten-free, casein-free soy milk

¼ cup cocoa

2¼ cups powdered sugar

1. In a food processor, combine shortening, margarine, vanilla, and 2 tablespoons soy milk.

2. Add powdered sugar and cocoa and combine until smooth.

3. If frosting is too thick, add remaining soy milk and process until smooth.

MAKES 2½ CUPS (FROSTS 12 CUPCAKES)

Calories: 131 | Fat: 4 g | Protein: 0 g | Fiber: 1 g

Vanilla Frosting

You can add gluten-free, casein-free food coloring to this vanilla frosting to create multicolored treats.

INGREDIENTS

2 tablespoons gluten-free, casein-free shortening

2 tablespoons gluten-free, casein-free margarine

1½ teaspoons gluten-free vanilla

2–3 tablespoons gluten-free, casein-free soy milk

2¼ cups powdered sugar

1. In a food processor, combine shortening, margarine, vanilla, and 2 tablespoons soy milk.

2. Add in powdered sugar, and blend until smooth. If the frosting is too thick, add more soy milk.

MAKES 2½ CUPS

Calories: 127 | Fat: 4 g | Protein: 0 g | Fiber: 0 g

Cherry Apple Coconut Rice Pudding

Since frozen cherries already have the pits removed, using them dramatically limits the prep time in this dish. You can make this dish a little lighter with light coconut milk if needed.

INGREDIENTS

1 cup Arborio rice

1 (15-ounce) can coconut milk

1 cup frozen cherries, thawed

1 cup chunky applesauce

1. Preheat oven to 325°F.

2. Rinse rice.

3. Combine all ingredients in a covered casserole.

4. Bake 1 hour.

MAKES 4 CUPS (4 SERVINGS)

Calories: 444 | Fat: 23 g | Protein: 6 g | Fiber: 3 g

Chocolate Chip Cookies

If you don't like the flavor of coconut oil, you can substitute gluten-free, casein-free margarine.

INGREDIENTS

3 cups gluten-free all-purpose flour

1 teaspoon xanthan gum

1 teaspoon baking soda

½ teaspoon salt

½ cup applesauce

½ teaspoon baking powder

¾ cup coconut oil

1½ cups packed dark brown sugar

1 tablespoon gluten-free vanilla

2 cups gluten-free, casein-free chocolate chips

Why Use Coconut Oil?

Coconut oil is solid at room temperature, making it a great substitute for butter in dairy-free baking. It also has a slightly sweet, coconutty flavor that contributes to yummy baked goods. Because of its flavor, it also works well with many ethnic flavors, like Asian or Caribbean cooking.

1. Preheat oven to 375°F.

2. In a medium bowl, combine flour, xanthan gum, baking soda, and salt.

3. In a separate bowl, combine applesauce and baking powder.

4. Add coconut oil, brown sugar, and vanilla to applesauce mixture.

5. Beat wet ingredients together using an electric mixer for 1–2 minutes, or until well combined.

6. Blend dry ingredients into wet.

7. Mix in chocolate chips.

8. Drop batter by the tablespoon onto ungreased cookie sheets.

9. Bake 10–12 minutes or until golden brown.

10. Remove cookies from cookie sheets, and cool on cooling racks.

MAKES 60 COOKIES (SERVING = 3 COOKIES)

Calories: 246 | Fat: 14 g | Protein: 3 g | Fiber: 3 g

Hot Chocolate

*Add an ice cube or two to make hot chocolate
"not quite so hot" for sensitive mouths.
Top with gluten-free, casein-free marshmallows for a fun wintery treat.*

INGREDIENTS

1 tablespoon agave nectar

2 teaspoons cocoa

½ teaspoon gluten-free vanilla

1 cup gluten-free, casein-free soy milk

1. In an empty coffee cup, combine agave nectar, cocoa, and vanilla.

2. In a small saucepan, heat soy milk until hot, but not boiling.

3. Add milk to chocolate mixture.

MAKES 1 CUP

Calories: 173 | Fat: 2 g | Protein: 2 g | Fiber: 4 g

Where's the Gluten in Vanilla?

Vanilla extract is usually the result of vanilla beans that have been soaked in alcohol. For a vanilla to be gluten-free, it must have been extracted using an alcohol derived from a nonglutinous grain. If a vanilla doesn't say that it's gluten-free, choose another brand.

Lemon Raspberry Ice Pops

*Vitamin C takes a refreshing turn
in this sweet treat.*

INGREDIENTS

½ cup lemonade

½ cup raspberry puree

1. Combine lemonade and raspberry puree.
2. Pour into a clean, empty ice cube tray.
3. Cover ice cube tray with aluminum foil or plastic wrap.
4. Poke a craft stick through a slit in each of the filled ice cube spots.
5. Freeze until solid and remove foil or plastic wrap.
6. If it is difficult to get the pops out of the tray, run the bottom of the ice cube tray under warm water to loosen.

MAKES 3 ICE POPS

Calories: 110 | Fat: 0 g | Protein: 0 g | Fiber: 1 g

Limeade Sorbet

Keeping clean grapes in a freezer-safe container makes them accessible not only for this dessert, but also as a sweet frozen treat on their own.

INGREDIENTS

1½ cups prepared limeade from frozen concentrate

¾ cup frozen white grapes

Limeade, Lemonade

Limeade, and its more popular sister, lemonade, are made from mixing the juice of either limes or lemons, sweetener, and water or other juice. Different proportions yield sweeter or tarter results, but try this for a starting place: ¼ cup lime or lemon juice, 2 cups white grape juice, 1 teaspoon agave nectar. Combine all ingredients and stir. Serve over ice.

1. Combine ingredients in a blender or food processor; blend until smooth.

2. Pour into a freezer-safe container.

3. Freeze for 2 hours, then fluff with a fork.

4. Return to freezer.

5. Continue fluffing every 1½–2 hours until serving.

MAKES 2¼ CUPS (SERVES 4)

Calories: 280 | Fat: 0 g | Protein: 0 g | Fiber: 0 g

Mango Honeydew Sorbet

*Sweet honeydew and flavorful mango combine
for an interesting frozen combination.*

INGREDIENTS

½ medium honeydew

1½ cups mango chunks

½ cup apple juice

1. In a food processor or blender, puree all ingredients together.

2. Pour into a freezer-safe container.

3. After 1½–2 hours, fluff sorbet with a fork, then return to freezer.

4. After 2 hours, fluff sorbet with a fork.

5. Continue fluffing every 2 hours until ready to serve.

SERVES 4

Calories: 99 | Fat: 0 g | Protein: 1 g | Fiber: 2 g

Orange Coconut Sorbet

Sweet and creamy, this dessert adds important fat and vitamin C.

INGREDIENTS

2 cups orange juice

1 cup coconut milk

Softening Sorbet

Sorbet can harden if left in the freezer overnight. Take sorbet out of the freezer and let sit on the counter for 5 minutes to allow it to soften before serving.

1. Combine juice and milk.

2. Pour into a covered freezer-safe container.

3. After 1½–2 hours, fluff with a fork, and return to freezer.

4. Continue fluffing every 2 hours until ready to serve.

MAKES 3 CUPS (3 SERVINGS)

Calories: 223 | Fat: 16 g | Protein: 3 g | Fiber: 0 g

Apple Pear Crisp

This fruity dessert is great served with some gluten-free, casein-free soy ice cream on top!

INGREDIENTS

3 medium pears

3 large apples

¾ cup packed light brown sugar

1 teaspoon gluten-free vanilla

½ cup gluten-free all-purpose flour

¼ cup gluten-free, casein-free rolled oats

½ teaspoon xanthan gum

¼ cup butter or gluten-free, casein-free margarine, melted

Canola oil spray

1. Preheat oven to 400°F.

2. Peel and thinly slice pears and apples.

3. In a small bowl combine remaining ingredients.

4. Spray a 2-quart casserole with canola oil.

5. Spread fruit in bottom of casserole.

6. Top with sugar mixture.

7. Bake 40 minutes.

MAKES 4 CUPS (8 SERVINGS)

Calories: 229 | Fat: 6 g | Protein: 2 g | Fiber: 4 g

Pineapple Coconut Rice Pudding

With these three ingredients in the pantry, making this tasty, wholesome dessert is a snap.

INGREDIENTS

1 (15-ounce) can coconut milk

1 (15-ounce) can crushed
   pineapple in juice

1 cup Arborio rice

1. Preheat oven to 325°F.

2. In a small saucepan, bring coconut milk and crushed pineapple with juice to a boil.

3. Rinse rice.

4. Combine rice with liquid in a covered casserole.

5. Bake 1 hour.

MAKES 4 CUPS (8 SERVINGS)

Calories: 217 | Fat: 11 g | Protein: 3 g | Fiber: 1 g

Strawberry Cantaloupe Sorbet

Since this frozen treat has no added sugar, it can be served as a healthy snack on a hot day, as well as a dessert.

INGREDIENTS

½ medium cantaloupe

1½ cups strawberries

½ cup apple juice

Pyrex Casserole Dishes Are Not Just for Baking

A covered Pyrex casserole is the ideal container for making sorbet. The shallow rectangle shape makes it easy to store sorbet in a crowded freezer. Furthermore, the easy-to-remove lids keep freezer odors out, while keeping liquid in. An added bonus is that colorful sorbet looks great in a glass container, leading to an impressive display while serving tableside. If Pyrex isn't available, a stainless steel mixing bowl covered with aluminum foil works well, too.

1. In a food processor or blender, puree all ingredients together.
2. Pour into a freezer-safe container.
3. After 1½–2 hours, fluff sorbet with a fork, then return to freezer.
4. Every 2 hours, fluff sorbet with a fork.
5. Continue this process until ready to serve.

MAKES 4 CUPS (4 SERVINGS)

Calories: 67 | Fat: 0 g | Protein: 1 g | Fiber: 2 g

Vanilla Maple Rice Pudding

*Serve a scoop of this pudding warmed
with some blueberries on the side.*

INGREDIENTS

1 cup Arborio rice

4 cups gluten-free, casein-free
soy milk

½ cup pure maple syrup

2 tablespoons gluten-free vanilla

Vanilla, the Tropical Flower

Vanilla beans come from a member of the orchid family. They originated in Mexico, but are widely grown throughout the tropics, especially in Madagascar. The beautiful flavor and aroma of the vanilla bean is used in baked goods, confections, and perfumes around the world.

1. Preheat oven to 325°F.

2. Rinse rice.

3. In a small saucepan, bring soy milk, maple syrup, and vanilla to a boil.

4. Combine liquid and rice in a covered 2-quart casserole.

5. Bake 1 hour.

MAKES 4 CUPS (8 SERVINGS)

Calories: 197 | Fat: 1 g | Protein: 4 g | Fiber: 2 g

Vanilla Raspberry Sorbet

*For a seedless sorbet, press mixture through
a fine-mesh sieve before freezing.*

INGREDIENTS

2 cups raspberries

1½ teaspoons gluten-free vanilla

3 tablespoons apple juice
concentrate

Raspberries and Blackberries, a Black Belt in Good Health

Both raspberries and blackberries are rich with antioxidants. Antioxidants are believed to protect your body's cells from damage caused by tobacco, radiation, and even the unhealthy by-products of food you eat.

1. Puree all ingredients in a food processor or blender.

2. Pour into a freezer-safe container.

3. Freeze for 2 hours, then fluff with a fork.

4. Return to freezer.

5. Continue fluffing every 1½–2 hours until serving.

MAKES 2¼ CUPS (2 SERVINGS)

Calories: 107 | Fat: 1 g | Protein: 1 g | Fiber: 8 g

Chocolate Nut Clusters

There is no reason to go without special-occasion treats when making your own candies is so easy and delicious.

INGREDIENTS

1 cup gluten-free, casein-free chocolate chips

1 cup cashew pieces (or other nut, like pecans or walnuts)

1. Fill a mini muffin pan with muffin papers.

2. Heat chocolate chips over medium-low flame, stirring constantly until almost completely melted.

3. Remove from heat and continue stirring until chocolate is completely melted.

4. Stir nuts into melted chocolate.

5. Use a teaspoon to fill muffin papers.

6. Refrigerate candies for at least 1½ hours.

MAKES 16 CANDIES

Calories: 103 | Fat: 7 g | Protein: 2 g | Fiber: 1 g

Chocolate Coconut Brownies

These brownies are a great treat to bring as a potluck dessert.
The coconut gives it an excellent flavor and texture!

INGREDIENTS

¾ teaspoon light brown sugar

½ cup coconut oil

1½ teaspoons gluten-free vanilla

1 (12-ounce) package gluten-free, casein-free chocolate chips

1¼ cups gluten-free all-purpose flour

1 tablespoon xanthan gum

½ teaspoon baking soda

½ teaspoon salt

½ cup applesauce

½ teaspoon baking powder

½ cup finely shredded coconut

No Microwave? No Problem!

If you don't have a microwave to make these brownies, that's no problem. Heat the coconut oil and brown sugar in a small saucepan, stirring continuously until the coconut oil is melted.

1. Preheat oven to 350°F.

2. Combine brown sugar and coconut oil in a large microwave-safe bowl. Microwave on high for 1–2 minutes until coconut oil is melted.

3. Stir oil and brown sugar, mix in the vanilla and half the chocolate chips. Set aside.

4. In a medium bowl, combine flour, xanthan gum, baking soda, and salt.

5. In a small bowl, combine applesauce and baking powder. Mix applesauce mixture into coconut oil–chocolate mixture.

6. Mix dry ingredients into wet. Stir remaining chocolate chips and shredded coconut into batter.

7. Lightly oil an 8- or 9-inch-square pan with coconut oil. Spoon batter into pan. Bake 35 minutes or until a toothpick inserted into the center comes out clean. Cool completely before cutting.

MAKES 12 BROWNIES

Calories: 302 | Fat: 19 g | Protein: 4 g | Fiber: 3 g

Golden Marshmallow Treats

Get creative with this as a base! Add different nut butters, or experiment with different dried fruits such as dried apricots, strawberries, or even gluten-free, casein-free chocolate!

INGREDIENTS

8 tablespoons gluten-free, casein-free margarine

10 ounces gluten-free and vegan Rice Mellow Crème or gluten-free, casein-free marshmallows

6 cups Rice Chex

¼ cup peanut butter (optional)

½ cup golden raisins

1. Melt the margarine in a large skillet over medium-low heat.

2. Add the Rice Mellow Crème and stir frequently until they are melted together.

3. Add the Rice Chex, peanut butter, and raisins.

4. Stir until all of the ingredients are thoroughly coated.

5. Spread the Rice Chex mixture into a greased 9" × 13" casserole dish.

6. Allow to cool. Cut into squares and serve.

MAKES 12 TREATS

Calories: 237 | Fat: 10 g | Protein: 2 g | Fiber: 1 g

Chocolate-Coated Strawberries

Keep these strawberries in the refrigerator until ready to serve;
they will start to melt in a warm room.

INGREDIENTS

16 fresh strawberries with leaves
attached

⅔ cup gluten-free, casein-free
chocolate chips

1. Wash strawberries, and let them dry completely.

2. In a small saucepan, partially melt chocolate chips over medium heat, stirring constantly.

3. Once halfway melted, remove from heat, and continue stirring until completely melted.

4. Dip strawberries, one at a time, in the melted chocolate.

5. Place coated strawberries on a wax-paper-covered cookie sheet.

6. Refrigerate strawberries for at least ½ hour before serving.

MAKES 16 STRAWBERRIES

Calories: 43 | Fat: 2 g | Protein: 1 g | Fiber: 1 g

Chocolate Pudding

Although prepared gluten- and casein-free puddings are available at the grocery store, it's great to be able to make this creamy treat with ingredients that are often on hand.

INGREDIENTS

¼ cup gluten-free, casein-free cocoa

¼ cup sugar

1½ teaspoons gluten-free vanilla

¼ cup water, divided

2 tablespoons cornstarch

1 cup gluten-free, casein-free soy milk

1 cup gluten-free, casein-free rice milk

Don't Boil That Soy Milk!

Soy milk should not come to a full boil, as it alters the flavor. If you are preparing a recipe that calls for a boiled milk alternative try rice milk or a nut milk instead.

1. In a small bowl, mix cocoa, sugar, and vanilla. Add hot water, 1 tablespoon at a time until dissolved into a thick paste.

2. In a separate bowl, mix cornstarch and 2 tablespoons cold water until dissolved.

3. Heat soy milk and rice milk in a medium saucepan over medium heat.

4. Add chocolate paste and stir until completely dissolved.

5. When chocolate mixture is at a high simmer, just before boiling, add cornstarch mixture, reduce heat, and stir continuously until thickened.

6. Transfer pudding to bowls and refrigerate.

YIELDS 2½ CUPS (5 SERVINGS)

Calories: 317 | Fat: 1 g | Protein: 2 g | Fiber: 2 g

CHAPTER 13

Odds and Ends

Basic Applesauce

Sweeter apples like Golden Delicious will yield a sweeter applesauce, while tarter apples such as Granny Smith will result in an applesauce with a little more kick.

INGREDIENTS

2½ cups chopped, peeled apples

½ teaspoon cinnamon, optional

Thick or Thin?

While chunky applesauce can be great as a snack, smooth applesauce is what you should use for baking. To get that great chunky texture, stir the warm applesauce with a wooden spoon just enough to break up the really big chunks. To make smooth applesauce, transfer chunky applesauce to a blender or food processor and blend until smooth.

1. Place apple chunks in a large saucepan.

2. Sprinkle on cinnamon if using.

3. Cover apples with water.

4. Bring to a high simmer over medium-high heat.

5. Cook until apples break apart and are very soft. Remove from heat and stir to break up any large chunks.

MAKES 2 CUPS

Calories: 81 | Fat: 0 g | Protein: 0 g | Fiber: 4 g

Baked Tortilla Chips

Experiment with other types of gluten-free tortillas instead of corn for an interesting variation.

INGREDIENTS

5 corn tortillas

Canola oil

Sea salt

Some Snacking Ideas

Not every morsel that goes into your child's mouth is likely to be homemade. There are some great snacks that can make being out and about a little easier. Here are some ideas: Fruit cups, gluten-free pretzels, rice or corn cereal mixed with raisins, applesauce cups, allergen-free snack bars (gluten- and casein-free).

1. Preheat oven to 350°F.

2. Cut tortillas into 8 wedges each.

3. Spread oil on cookie sheet with a brush.

4. Spread tortilla wedges on cookie sheet in a single layer.

5. Brush tops of tortilla wedges with oil and sprinkle with salt.

6. Bake 13–15 minutes, until golden and crispy.

MAKES 40 CHIPS (5 SERVINGS)

Calories: 60 | Fat: 2 g | Protein: 1 g | Fiber: 2 g

Cinnamon Soy Yogurt Fruit Dip

Children love to dip, and this is a quick and easy yogurt dip that can be used with fruit or with vegetables! Using dips is a great way to increase your children's intake of healthy fruits and vegetables.

INGREDIENTS

1 (8-ounce) container gluten-free, casein-free vanilla soy yogurt

2 teaspoons wildflower honey or agave nectar

½ teaspoon cinnamon

1. Combine and stir the ingredients until smooth.

2. Drizzle over fruit or use as a dip.

YIELDS 1 CUP

Calories: 238 | Fat: 4 g | Protein: 8 g | Fiber: 2 g

Cinnamon Is More Than a Good-Tasting Spice!

Researchers have shown that ½ teaspoon of cinnamon per day may help to lower blood glucose in people with type 2 diabetes and may also help to control cholesterol and help improve brain function. Use cinnamon daily in your family meals or stick a cinnamon stick in teas or juice.

Trail Mix

*Take along this iron- and protein-rich snack
to stave off hunger pangs when on the go.*

INGREDIENTS

½ cup almond slices

½ cup sunflower seeds

½ cup dried cherries

½ cup raisins

3 tablespoons gluten-free, casein-
free chocolate chips (optional)

Combine all ingredients.

MAKES 2 CUPS (4 SERVINGS)

Calories: 385 │ Fat: 22 g │ Protein: 9 g │ Fiber: 6 g

Easy Gravy

Dips and sauces can make it easier to tempt picky palates. Use gravies, sauces, and dips to dress up steamed vegetables, broiled meats or tofu, or fruits.

INGREDIENTS

1 gluten-free, casein-free bouillon cube (vegetable, chicken, or beef)

1 cup plus 2 tablespoons water

2 teaspoons soy sauce

¼ teaspoon poultry seasoning

1 tablespoon cornstarch

Sensory Issues at the Table

Children who are sensitive to texture might be willing to give an otherwise unacceptable food a try if it's served with something appealing. Try serving a wide variety of foods with a favorite sauce or dip. Although ketchup-dipped cantaloupe might not be your cup of tea, it just might get some important nutrients past your child's lips.

1. Dissolve bouillon cube in 1 cup boiling water.

2. Add soy sauce and poultry seasoning to bouillon.

3. In a separate small bowl, thoroughly combine cornstarch with 2 tablespoons cold water.

4. Add diluted cornstarch to other mixture, stirring until combined and thickened.

MAKES 1 CUP

Calories: 45 | Fat: 0 g | Protein: 2 g | Fiber: 0 g

Guacamole

Omit the serrano pepper for a mild guacamole.

INGREDIENTS

2 avocados

½ medium onion

1 medium tomato

2 tablespoons cilantro

1 serrano pepper

1 tablespoon lime juice

1. Mash avocados with a potato masher or fork.

2. Finely chop onion, tomato, and cilantro.

3. Remove seeds from serrano pepper and finely mince.

4. Mix all ingredients.

MAKES 2 CUPS (4 SERVINGS)

Calories: 174 | Fat: 15 g | Protein: 3 g | Fiber: 8 g

Thank You, Aztec Civilization

Guacamole was invented by the Aztec people. It is believed that the higher fat content of the avocado was an important part of the otherwise relatively low-fat Aztec diet. The mash that we know of today is surprisingly similar to what the Aztecs savored in their day.

Hummus

To increase the spiciness of this dish, add one or two cloves of pressed garlic or ¼ teaspoon of cayenne pepper.

INGREDIENTS

2 cups cooked garbanzo beans (homemade or canned)

2 teaspoons lemon juice

3 tablespoons olive oil

1 clove garlic

¼ teaspoon cumin

⅛ teaspoon salt

1. If using canned garbanzo beans, drain and rinse beans.

2. Combine all ingredients in a food processor or blender.

3. Process until smooth.

YIELDS 2 CUPS

Calories: 234 | Fat: 12 g | Protein: 6 g | Fiber: 5 g

Hummus Yogurt Dipping Sauce

*This yogurt hummus tastes great when served with homemade
Baked Tortilla Chips, which are found on page 235.
Or serve with fresh vegetables for dipping.*

INGREDIENTS

1 (15-ounce) can garbanzo beans

1–2 cloves crushed garlic

1 tablespoon lemon juice

½ cup plus 1 tablespoon plain
    gluten-free, casein-free soy
    yogurt

1 teaspoon sea salt

½ teaspoon cumin

1. Drain can of beans and save liquid.

2. In a food processor, combine all
   ingredients and blend well.

3. Use liquid from garbanzo beans to
   thin to desired consistency.

YIELDS 2½ CUPS (5 SERVINGS)

Calories: 128 | Fat: 1 g | Protein: 5 g | Fiber: 4 g

Pineapple Salsa

Grilled pineapple can make a nice addition to this salsa. Cut a fresh pineapple into ½-inch-thick slices. Place on medium-hot grill and grill for 5–7 minutes per side. Allow to cool before using in cold salsa dish.

INGREDIENTS

1 cup diced fresh pineapple

½ cup red pepper, diced

½ cup yellow pepper, diced

½ cup black beans, drained and rinsed

¼ cup red onion, diced

¼ cup cilantro, finely chopped

¼ cup orange-pineapple juice

2 tablespoons lime juice

Salt and pepper to taste

1. In large bowl, combine first 6 ingredients and mix well.

2. In small bowl, combine orange-pineapple juice and lime juice. Pour into large bowl.

3. Mix all ingredients together; season with salt and pepper to taste.

YIELDS 4 CUPS (4 SERVINGS)

Calories: 70 | Fat: 0 g | Protein: 3 g | Fiber: 4 g

Refried Pinto Beans

This is a mild version of a Mexican classic dish.
To spice it up, you can add either seeded, chopped fresh jalapeño
or canned chopped jalapeño.

INGREDIENTS

1 cup dried pinto beans
  (or 1 [15-ounce] can)

1 tablespoon olive oil

½ onion

1 clove garlic

1 teaspoon cumin

1. If using dried beans, soak 6–8 hours or overnight before cooking.

2. Drain soaking water from beans, rinse, and combine beans with 3–4 cups water. Bring to a simmer with lid tilted.

3. Cook 1–1½ hours or until tender.

4. Drain and rinse either cooked beans or canned beans if using.

5. In a medium saucepan or sauté pan, heat olive oil over medium heat.

6. Add finely chopped onion and minced garlic.

7. Cook until onion is tender, 3–5 minutes.

8. Add beans and cumin and heat through.

9. Remove from heat and mash with a potato masher or fork.

MAKES 2 CUPS

Calories: 204 | Fat: 4 g | Protein: 11 g | Fiber: 8 g

Creamy Salsa Dip

This dip makes snack time fiesta time.
Serve with Baked Tortilla Chips (page 235) or veggie slices.
It also makes a nice base for a Mexican-style wrap sandwich.

INGREDIENTS

1 tablespoon gluten-free, casein-
   free soy cream cheese

1 tablespoon mild salsa

½ teaspoon agave nectar

1. Combine all ingredients.

2. Stir thoroughly.

MAKES 2 TABLESPOONS

Calories: 107 | Fat: 3 g | Protein: 1 g | Fiber: 1 g

Sweet Sunflower-Seed Butter Dip

Serve this sweet dipping sauce with cold steamed broccoli florets, baby carrots, or apple slices.

INGREDIENTS

1 tablespoon gluten-free, casein-free vanilla soy yogurt

1 tablespoon sunflower-seed butter

1 teaspoon agave nectar

1. Combine all ingredients in a small bowl.

2. Stir well.

MAKES 2 TABLESPOONS

Calories: 125 | Fat: 8 g | Protein: 4 g | Fiber: 0 g

Sweet Potato Spread

Serve this sweet spread to add vitamins to a slice of gluten-free toast or crackers.

INGREDIENTS

1 cup grated raw sweet potato

¾ cup water

1 teaspoon pure maple syrup

¼ teaspoon cinnamon

⅛ teaspoon nutmeg

2 tablespoons gluten-free, casein-free soy cream cheese

1. Bring sweet potato and water to a boil, keep boiling for 5 minutes.

2. Reduce heat to low and stir in remaining ingredients.

3. Keep stirring until cream cheese is melted and all ingredients are combined.

MAKES 1 CUP

Calories: 231 | Fat: 10 g | Protein: 4 g | Fiber: 4 g

Tropical Pudding Pie Dip

This tropical dip is a hit with kids!
Serve this dip with an arrangement of in-season fruit
to help your children try fruits that have not been tried before!

INGREDIENTS

1 small package dairy-free instant vanilla pudding

1½ cups gluten-free, casein-free soy milk

1 cup gluten-free, casein-free vanilla soy yogurt

⅓ cup orange-pineapple juice

½ teaspoon orange or lemon zest

1. Combine vanilla pudding and soy milk with a beater.

2. Once blended well, add remaining 3 ingredients and blend until smooth.

3. Chill and serve.

YIELDS 3 CUPS (3 SERVINGS)

Calories: 253 | Fat: 2 g | Protein: 5 g | Fiber: 1 g

A Different Way to Think about Soy Yogurt

When trying to adapt favorite recipes, it can be frustrating facing a long list of dairy ingredients. Soy yogurt can be a versatile team player. Try plain soy yogurt as a substitute for sour cream, or try sweetened, flavored soy yogurt in a recipe, like this one, with a sweet bent.

Yogurt Applesauce Dip

This dip works well for all kinds of fruit. It is easy to make in small batches or in large batches for family meals or gatherings.

INGREDIENTS

1 tablespoon applesauce

1 tablespoon gluten-free, casein-free vanilla soy yogurt

¼ teaspoon cinnamon

1. In a small bowl, combine all ingredients with a spoon.
2. Stir well.

MAKES 2 TABLESPOONS

Calories: 22 | Fat: 0 g | Protein: 1 g | Fiber: 0 g

Home-Style Gravy

This is a great basic gravy recipe that you can use to ladle over meats, chicken, and potatoes and other veggies. Substitute beef broth for chicken broth if you're serving the gravy with beef.

INGREDIENTS

½ teaspoon olive oil

½ cup chopped onion

1 teaspoon dried thyme

1½ tablespoons cornstarch

¼ cup water

1¼ cups gluten-free, casein-free chicken broth

¼ teaspoon salt

¼ teaspoon pepper

¼ teaspoon poultry seasoning

1. Coat a medium saucepan with olive oil and heat over medium-high heat. Add onion and dried thyme. Sauté until onion is tender, about 3 minutes.

2. Combine cornstarch and water in a small jar with a screw top. Shake until smooth and there are no lumps. Set aside.

3. Add broth to saucepan. Slowly stir in cornstarch mixture, stirring until smooth and well blended.

4. Add salt, pepper, and poultry seasoning to onion mixture. Bring to a boil, stirring constantly. Continue stirring and cooking until bubbly and thickened.

SERVES 12

Calories: 30 | Fat: 1 g | Protein: 1 g | Fiber: 0 g

Avocado Yogurt Dip

*This sweet and creamy dip can also be used
as a dressing for a green salad.*

INGREDIENTS

½ ripe avocado

¼ cup plain gluten-free, casein-
free soy yogurt

1 teaspoon agave nectar

2 tablespoons orange juice

1. Mash avocado with fork or potato masher.

2. Add remaining ingredients.

3. Stir until smooth.

MAKES 1 CUP

Calories: 323 | Fat: 17 g | Protein: 8 g | Fiber: 8 g

Fresh Croutons

These can be made in advance and stored in the refrigerator, then crisped up at the last moment. Double the recipe for extras.

INGREDIENTS

¼ cup olive oil

2 cloves garlic, minced or put through a garlic press

4 slices gluten-free, casein-free bread, thickly cut, crusts removed

Salt and pepper to taste

For the Love of Garlic

Garlic will give you various degrees of potency depending on how you cut it. Finely minced garlic, or that which has been put through a press, will be the strongest. When garlic is sliced, it is less strong, and when you leave the cloves whole, they are even milder.

1. Preheat the broiler to 350°F.

2. Mix the oil and garlic. Brush both sides of the bread with the garlic oil. Sprinkle with salt and pepper to taste.

3. Cut each slice of bread into 6 cubes to make 24 cubes. Spray a cookie sheet with olive oil. Place the cubes on the sheet and broil until well browned on both sides.

4. Put the cookie sheet on the bottom rack of the oven. Turn off the oven and leave the croutons to dry for 20 minutes.

5. Store in an airtight container until ready to use.

MAKES 24 CROUTONS (4 SERVINGS)

Calories: 196 | Fat: 17 g | Protein: 1 g | Fiber: 0 g

APPENDIX A
Resources for More Information

For More Information about Autism

The Centers for Disease Control, Autism Information Center
www.cdc.gov/ncbddd/autism

Medline Plus from the National Library of Medicine and the National
Institutes of Health
www.nlm.nih.gov/medlineplus/autism.html

National Institute of Mental Health
www.nimh.nih.gov/health/publications/autism-listing.shtml

For More Information about the Gluten- and Casein-Free Lifestyle

Celiac Sprue Association (for information and gluten-free resources)
www.csaceliacs.org

Celiac.com
www.celiac.com

Restaurant Guide
www.celiachandbook.com and *www.glutenfreerestaurants.org*

Living Without magazine
www.LivingWithout.com

Gluten- and Casein-Free Product Resources

Enjoy Life Foods
www.enjoylifefoods.com

Galaxy Nutritional Foods
www.galaxyfoods.com

Gluten Free Mall
www.glutenfreemall.com

Kinnikinnick Foods
www.kinnikinnick.com

Tinkyada
www.tinkyada.com

Tofutti
www.tofutti.com

Montina
www.montina.com

Whole Foods Gluten Free Bakehouse—Whole Foods Markets
www.wholefoodsmarket.com/products/gluten-free.php

School Meeting Worksheet

There are many things to think about before you meet with the staff of your child's school to discuss his diet. Use this worksheet as a brainstorming tool to help you prepare for questions you might be asked at school meetings.

1. What diet are you implementing? Is it a completely casein- and gluten-free diet? Are there any other restrictions or limitations?

2. How will you inform the school about changes in your child's diet? Will you provide them with written notice?

3. How will you communicate with the teacher and other school personnel about concerns over accidental exposures to casein and gluten?

4. What nonfood alternatives can you suggest for activities where food has traditionally been used in the classroom?

    - Reward charts
    - Stickers
    - Stamps
    - Beads, buttons, or cotton balls for counting and sorting activities
    - Bookmarks
    - "Good Job" certificates
    - Sequins, rickrack, craft sticks, buttons, or other craft items for assembling craft projects or decorating worksheets

5. What safe food alternatives for classroom activities can you suggest?

    - Gluten- and casein-free raisins or dried fruit
    - Rice- or corn-based cereal (ensuring that it is casein-free and gluten-free)

- Gluten- and casein-free popcorn
- Gluten- and casein-free candies or cookies

6. It can be really helpful to write a letter introducing your child and her dietary needs to the parents of children in her classroom. Include what you are willing to do to make it easier on them; one thing that can ease everyone's mind is asking if other parents will give you advance notice for when they are bringing food to school. That way, you can provide a safe alternative for your child on that day, and she won't have to feel excluded.

7. It is also a good idea to write a friendly letter to your child's teacher reiterating ideas for nonfood alternatives and safe-food alternatives to traditional classroom food-based activities. In this letter, also include what you are willing to do to make it easier for the teacher to support your child's diet. For example, you can volunteer in the classroom on days when there is going to be food (i.e., holiday parties), or you can provide a safe alternative for you child whenever you are given advance notice.

8. Ask your child's teacher if you can keep a box of safe snacks on hand for your child, in case a "treat" situation arises without advance notice. If your teacher has something safe to offer, you and he can feel more comfortable that exposures will not occur.

APPENDIX C

Sample Menus

Day 1

Breakfast:	Veggie Omelet	(Page 97)
	Old-Fashioned Biscuits	(Page 50)
	1 cup soy milk	
Snack:	Golden Marshmallow Treats	(Page 230)
Lunch:	Curried Chicken	(Page 179)
	GF Corn Tortillas	
	Fruit Salad	(Page 105)
Snack:	Trail Mix	(Page 237)
Dinner:	Fish Baked in Papillote	(Page 139)
	Roasted Winter Vegetables	(Page 200)
	Veggie Stuffing	(Page 203)
	1 cup soy milk	

Day 2

Breakfast:	Breakfast Pizza	(Page 76)
	1 cup calcium-fortified orange juice	
Snack:	Creamy Salsa Dip	(Page 244)
	Fresh vegetables cut up for dipping	
Lunch:	Hummus and Mango Sandwich	(Page 168)
	Homemade Potato Chips	(Page 181)
	Pink Soy Milk	(Page 84)
Snack:	Rice cake with sunflower-seed butter	
Dinner:	Barbecue Meatloaf Muffins	(Page 120)
	Roasted Potato Salad	(Page 110)
	Apple-Roasted Carrots	(Page 185)
	Broiled Pineapple with Vanilla Frozen Yogurt	(Page 209)

Day 3

Breakfast:	Blueberry and Banana Soy Yogurt with Crispy Rice	(Page 73)
Snack:	Pineapple Salsa	(Page 242)
	Corn chips	
Lunch:	Granola	(Page 74)
	Sliced bananas	
	1 cup soy milk	
Snack:	Sweet Potato Pie	(Page 210)
Dinner:	Black Bean Cakes	(Page 144)
	Citrusy Rice Salad	(Page 103)
	Corn tortillas	
	1 cup soy milk	

Day 4

Breakfast:	Sunflower-Seed Butter and Banana Smoothie	(Page 89)
Snack:	Sweet Potato Muffin	(Page 44)
Lunch:	Lentil Soup	(Page 59)
	Corny Cornbread	(Page 42)
	1 cup soy milk	
Snack:	Apple	
	1 cup soy milk	
Dinner:	Barbecue Tofu and Quinoa	(Page 143)
	Cucumber Tomato Salad	(Page 104)
	Fresh fruit	

Day 5

Breakfast:	Crispy Potato Pancakes	(Page 93)
	Scrambled eggs with cheese	
	1 cup soy milk	
Snack:	Strawberry Applesauce	(Page 85)
Lunch:	Tofu Bites	(Page 174)
	Black Bean Slaw	(Page 114)
Snack:	Fruit Kabobs	(Page 79)
Dinner:	Turkey Chili	(Page 67)
	Corny Cornbread	(Page 42)
	1 cup soy milk	

Day 6

Breakfast:	Tropical Fruit Smoothie	(Page 91)
Snack:	Zucchini Yacht	(Page 177)
	1 cup soy milk	
Lunch:	PB & J Muffins	(Page 53)
This lunch makes a great packed lunch for school!	GF corn chips	
	Juice Box or fresh fruit	
Snack:	Chocolate Chip Cookies	(Page 217)
	1 cup soy milk	
Dinner:	Taco Dinner	(Page 132)
	Refried Pinto Beans	(Page 243)

Day 7

Breakfast:	Good Morning Pancakes	(Page 92)
	1 cup soy milk	
Snack:	Avocado Yogurt Dip	(Page 250)
	Fresh vegetables cut up for dipping	
Lunch:	Turkey Cheese Roll-Up	(Page 175)
	Homemade Potato Chips	(Page 181)
	Mango Coleslaw	(Page 108)
Snack:	Lemon Raspberry Ice Pops	(Page 219)
Dinner:	Macaroni and Cheese	(Page 160)
	Mixed Vegetable Kabobs	(Page 206)
	Fresh fruit	
	1 cup soy milk	

Glossary of Basic Cooking Terms

Active dry yeast

This is a small plant that has been preserved by drying. When rehydrated, the yeast activates and begins producing carbon dioxide and alcohols.

Al dente

A term used in Italian cooking that refers to the texture of cooked pasta. When cooked "al dente," the pasta is tender, but still firm in the middle. The term literally means "to the tooth."

Bake

To cook in dry heat, usually in an oven, until proteins denature, starches gelatinize, and water evaporates to form a structure.

Beat

To combine two mixtures and to incorporate air by manipulating with a spoon or an electric mixer until fluffy.

Blanch

Blanching is a means of cooking food by immersing it in boiling water. After blanching, the cooked food is immediately placed in cold water to stop the cooking process. Always drain blanched foods thoroughly before adding to a dish.

Butter

A natural fat obtained by churning heavy cream to consolidate and remove some of the butterfat.

Calorie

A unit of measurement in nutrition, a calorie is the amount of energy needed to raise the temperature of 1 gram of water by 1 degree Celsius. The number of calories in a food is measured by chemically analyzing the food.

Casein

Protein found in milk and used independently in many foods as a bonding agent.

Cholesterol

Cholesterol is not a fat, but a sterol; an alcohol and fatty acid, a soft, waxy substance used by your body to make hormones. Your body makes cholesterol and you eat foods containing cholesterol. Only animal fats have cholesterol.

Chop

Chopping consists of cutting food into small pieces. While chopped food doesn't need to be perfectly uniform, the pieces should be roughly the same size.

Confectioner's sugar

This sugar is finely ground and mixed with cornstarch to prevent lumping; it is used mostly in icings and frostings. It is also known as powdered sugar and 10X sugar.

Corn oil

An oil obtained from the germ of the corn kernel. It has a high smoke point and contains a small amount of artificial trans fat.

Cornmeal

Coarsely ground corn, used to make polenta, also to coat foods to make a crisp crust.

Cornstarch

Very finely ground powder made from the starch in the endosperm of corn; used as a thickener.

Deep-fry

To fry in a large amount of oil or melted shortening, lard, or butter so the food is completely covered. In this dry-heat method of cooking, about 10 percent of the fat is absorbed into the food.

Dice

Dicing consists of cutting food into small cubes, usually ¼ inch in size or less. Unlike chopping, the food should be cut into even-sized pieces.

Dissolve

To immerse a solid in a liquid and heat or manipulate to form a solution in which none of the solid remains.

Drain

Draining consists of drawing off the liquid from a food. Either a colander (a perforated bowl made of metal or plastic) or paper towels can be used to drain food.

Dredge

To dip a food into another mixture, usually made of flour, bread crumbs, or cheese, to completely coat.

Edamame

The word for edible soybeans, a green pea encased in a pod.

Emulsify

To combine an oil and a liquid, either through manipulation or the addition of another ingredient, so they remain suspended in each other.

Fatty acid
A fatty acid is a long chain of carbon molecules bonded to each other and to hydrogen molecules, attached to an alcohol or glycerol molecule. They are short-chain, medium-chain, and long-chain, always with an even number of carbon molecules.

Flaky
A food texture, (usually describing a pie crust or crust on meat), which breaks apart into flat layers.

Flaxseed
This small, oil-rich seed is used primarily to make linseed oil, but is also a valuable source of nutrients like calcium, iron, and omega-3 fatty acids.

Fry
To cook food in hot oil, a dry-heat environment.

Gluten
A protein in flour made by combining glutenin and gliadin with a liquid via physical manipulation.

Golden
The color of food when it is browned or quickly sautéed.

HDL
High-density lipoproteins, the "good" type of cholesterol that carries fat away from the bloodstream.

Herbs
The aromatic leafy part of an edible plant; herbs include basil, parsley, chives, thyme, tarragon, oregano, and mint.

Hummus
A combination of puréed chickpeas with garlic, lemon juice, and usually tahini; used as an appetizer or sandwich spread.

Hydrogenation
The process of adding hydrogen molecules to carbon chains in fats and fatty acids.

Italian salad dressing
A dressing made of olive oil and vinegar or lemon juice, combined into an emulsion, usually with herbs like basil, oregano, and thyme.

Jelly
A congealed mixture made from fruit juice, sugar, and pectin.

Julienne
To julienne food (also called matchstick cutting) consists of cutting it into very thin strips about 1½ to 2 inches long, with a width and thickness of about ⅛ inch. Both meat and vegetables can be julienned.

Kabob
Meats, fruits, and/or vegetables threaded onto skewers, usually barbecued over a wood or coal fire.

Kidney bean
A legume, either white or dark red, used for making chili and soups.

Knead
To manipulate a dough, usually a bread dough, to help develop the gluten in the flour so the bread has the proper texture.

Lard
The fat from pork, used to fry foods and as a substitute for margarine or butter.

LDL
Low-density lipoproteins, the "bad" cholesterol, which carry fat from the liver and intestines to the bloodstream.

Lecithin
A fatty substance that is a natural emulsifier, found in eggs and legumes.

Lipid
Lipids are organic molecules insoluble in water, consisting of a chain of hydrophobic carbon and hydrogen molecules and an alcohol or glycerol molecule. They include fats, oil, waxes, steroids, and cholesterol.

Long-chain fatty acids
These fatty acids have twelve to twenty-four carbon molecules bonded to hydrogen molecules and to a glycerol molecule.

Margarine
A fat made by hydrogenating polyunsaturated oils, colored with yellow food coloring to resemble butter.

Marinate
To coat foods in an acidic liquid or dry mixture to help break down protein bonds and tenderize the food.

Mayonnaise
An emulsification of egg yolks, lemon juice or vinegar, and oil, blended into a thick white creamy dressing.

Meat thermometer
A thermometer specially labeled to read the internal temperature of meat.

Medium-chain fatty acids
These fatty acids have six to twelve carbon molecules bonded to each other and to hydrogen molecules. Coconut and palm oils contain these fatty acids, which are used in infant formulas.

Mince
Mincing consists of cutting food into very small pieces. In general, minced food is cut into smaller pieces than diced food.

Monounsaturated oil
A fatty acid that has two carbons double-bonded to each other, missing two hydrogen molecules. These very stable oils are good for frying but can have low smoke points. Examples include olive, almond, avocado, canola, and peanut oils.

Mortar and pestle
A mortar is a bowl-shaped tool, sometimes made of stone or marble, and a pestle is the round instrument used to grind ingredients in the mortar.

Mouthfeel
A food science term that describes the action of food in the mouth; descriptors range from gummy to dry to slippery to smooth to chewy to tender.

Nuts
The edible fruit of some trees, consisting of a kernel in a hard shell. Most edible nuts are actually seeds and are a good source of monounsaturated fats.

Omega-3 fatty acids
A polyunsaturated fat named for the position of the first double bond. The body cannot make omega-3 fatty acids; they must be consumed.

Omega-6 fatty acids
A polyunsaturated fat name for the position of the first double bond. Too much of this fatty acid in the body can cause heart disease. Like HDL with LDL cholesterol, it works in concert with omega-3 fatty acids.

Organic food
Food that has been grown and processed without pesticides, herbicides, insecticides, fertilizers, artificial coloring, artificial flavoring, or additives.

Pan-fry
To quickly fry a food item in a small amount of oil in a saucepan or skillet.

Polyunsaturated oil
A fatty acid that has more than two carbon molecules double-bonded to each other; it is missing at least four hydrogen molecules. Examples include corn, soybean, safflower, and sunflower oils.

Processed food
Any food that has been manipulated by chemicals or otherwise treated, such as frozen food, canned food, enriched foods, and dehydrated foods.

Rancid
Over time, and through exposure to oxygen, fats oxidize, or break down, and free radicals form, which then exacerbate the breakdown process. Rancid fats smell and taste unpleasant.

Reduction
Quickly boiling or simmering liquid to evaporate the water and concentrate the flavor.

Risotto
An Italian rice dish made by slowly cooking rice in broth, stirring to help release starch that thickens the mixture.

Roast
To cook food at relatively high heat in an oven. This is a dry-cooking method, usually used for vegetables and meats.

Roux
A mixture of flour and oil or fat, cooked until the starches in the flour can absorb liquid. It is used to thicken sauces, from white sauce to gumbo.

Saturated fat
A fatty acid that has no double-bonded carbons but has all the carbons bonded to hydrogen molecules. Butter, coconut oil, and palm oil are all high in saturated fats.

Sauté
To quickly cook food in a small amount of fat over relatively high heat.

Sear
Searing meat consists of quickly browning it over high heat before finishing cooking it by another method. Searing meat browns the surface and seals in the juices.

Season
To change the flavor of food by adding ingredients like salt, pepper, herbs, and spices.

Short-chain fatty acid
A fat that contains two to six carbon molecules; examples include lauric and octanoic acids.

Shortening
A partially hydrogenated oil that is solid at room temperature, used to make everything from frostings to cakes to pastries and breads.

Shred
Shredding food consists of cutting it into thin strips that are usually thicker than a julienne cut. Meat, poultry, cabbage, lettuce, and cheese can all be shredded.

Simmer
Simmering food consists of cooking it in liquid at a temperature just below the boiling point.

Smoke point
The temperature at which fats begin to break down under heat. The higher the smoke point, the more stable the fat will be while frying and cooking. Butter's smoke point is 350°F, olive oil 375°F, and refined oils around 440°F.

Spices
Aromatic seasonings from seeds, bark, roots, and stems of edible plants. Spices include cinnamon, cumin, turmeric, ginger, and pepper, among others.

Trans
Latin word meaning "across," referring to the positioning of the hydrogen molecules on the carbon chain of a fatty acid.

Trans fat
A specific form of fatty acid where hydrogen molecules are positioned across from each other, in the "trans" position, as opposed to the "cis" position.

Tropical oils
Oils from plants grown in the tropic regions; the most common are coconut oil and palm oil. These oils are usually fully saturated and are solid at room temperature.

Unsalted butter
Sometimes known as "sweet butter," this is butter that contains no salt or sodium chloride. It's used for greasing pans, since salt in butter will make batter or dough stick.

Unsaturated fat
Fatty acids that have two or more carbon molecules double-bonded to each other; an unsaturated fat is missing at least two hydrogen molecules.

Vanilla
The highly aromatic seeds contained in a long pod, or fruit, of the vanilla plant, a member of the orchid family.

Vegetable oil
Oils made by pressing or chemically extracting lipids from a vegetable source, whether seeds, nuts, or fruits of a plant.

Vitamins
Vitamins are molecules that are used to promote and facilitate chemical reactions in the body. Most vitamins must be ingested as your body cannot make them.

Index

Note: Page numbers in **bold** indicate recipe category lists.